The ESSENTIALS® of

Business Statistics I

Louise J. Clark, Ph.D.
Professor of Business Statistics
Jacksonville State University, Jacksonville, AL

This book covers the usual course outline of Business Statistics I. For more advanced topics, see *"THE ESSENTIALS OF BUSINESS STATISTICS II."*

Research & Education Association
61 Ethel Road West
Piscataway, New Jersey 08854

THE ESSENTIALS®
OF BUSINESS STATISTICS I

Year 2003 Printing

Printed in the United States of America

Library of Congress Control Number 00-132035

International Standard Book Number 0-87891-841-8

ESSENTIALS is a registered trademark of
Research & Education Association, Piscataway, New Jersey 08854

WHAT "THE ESSENTIALS" WILL DO FOR YOU

This book is a review and study guide. It is comprehensive and it is concise.

It helps in preparing for exams and in doing homework, and remains a handy reference source at all times.

It condenses the vast amount of detail characteristic of the subject matter and summarizes the **essentials** of the field.

It will thus save hours of study and preparation time.

The book provides quick access to the important facts, principles, and concepts in the field.

Materials needed for exams can be reviewed in summary form— eliminating the need to read and re-read many pages of textbook and class notes. The summaries will even tend to bring detail to mind that had been previously read or noted.

This "ESSENTIALS" book has been prepared by an expert in the field, and has been carefully reviewed to ensure accuracy and maximum usefulness.

Dr. Max Fogiel
Program Director

CONTENTS

CHAPTER 1

INTRODUCTION

1.1 DEFINITION OF STATISTICS

STATISTICS is defined as the process of collecting, analyzing, interpreting, and presenting data. A distinction should be made between "statistics" as a science or course of study and the term "statistic" which we are accustomed to hearing when listening to the sports news broadcast or the weather report, for example. The term "statistic" is the final outcome (number) which is derived from the science of "statistics" or "statistical methods."

Statistical methods are categorized as:

a) **Descriptive** - that body of techniques which describes a set of data in an effort to condense or better understand what is there (e.g., the average age of a group of 100 individuals might give one a much better image of the group as compared to an individual listing of each of the 100 ages).

b) **Inferential** - that body of techniques which allows us to draw conclusions about a larger group of objects by examining only a portion of those objects (e.g., predicting the outcome of an election by taking a random sample of registered voters).

1.2   STATISTICS IN BUSINESS

Statistical data serve as a general aid to the managerial decision making process. One cannot make wise decisions without a proper understanding of the facts used in making those decisions. The most successful decision makers are people who can most effectively make use of the information which is available to them. In some instances, statistical data are collected for a particular purpose, such as a decision on the feasibility of marketing a new product, while in other instances, general information might be sought about economic conditions. Statistical methods are applied to answer questions in all of the major business disciplines including accounting, finance, marketing, economics, production, and of course, general management.

1.3   TYPES OF STATISTICAL DATA

DATA are the facts on which we perform statistical methods or techniques; i.e., facts which we collect, analyze, interpret, and present. Data are either:

   a) **qualitative** - verbal; e.g., gender, race, class in school,

                           or

   b) **quantitative** - numerical; e.g., height, weight, age, or score on
                           an exam.

If data are qualitative, we may analyze them by determining the percentage falling within each category. For example, if we are analyzing information about the gender mix of a group, we may express this either as the total of males and females in the group or the percentage of males and females in the group. Other methods of attempting to "make sense" of this characteristic would yield useless results. On the other hand, the types of analysis that can be performed on quantitative data are much broader and will be the basis for most of the material presented in this book. It should be noted, however, that qualitative data are often coded as numerical data (e.g., male = 1 and female = 2) in order to permit certain forms of quantitative analysis.

2

1.4 SOURCES OF STATISTICAL DATA

Data may be collected from a number of different sources.

Internal Data are facts that are collected from records of the organization desiring the data; e.g., company records such as sales figures, inventory records, payroll information.

External Data are facts that are collected from sources outside the organization desiring the information; i.e., from sources other than company records. These data are published and may be in the form of a:

> **Primary Source** - that which presents data collected and published first hand
>
> or
>
> **Secondary Source** - that which republishes data taken from a previously published source.

On the other hand, external data may be collected from an original investigation utilizing a survey technique. When this is the case, these data are referred to as **Primary Data**.

CHAPTER 2

DESCRIPTIVE STATISTICS

2.1 FREQUENCY DISTRIBUTIONS AND GRAPHS/CHARTS

A frequency distribution is one method of condensing original data into a more usable form. It is a table which is used to summarize a set of data by showing the number of items contained in the individual categories set forth in the table. A frequency distribution may be constructed using either qualitative or quantitative data. Qualitative data are much easier to tabulate in this manner due to the natural categorization of the data.

a) Qualitative Data

Frequency distributions illustrating qualitative data simply indicate the categories into which the data are to be divided and the number (or percentage) of the objects falling within each category.

EXAMPLE:

FREQUENCY DISTRIBUTION
OF THE NUMBER OF STUDENTS
ENROLLED IN XYZ UNIVERSITY
BROKEN DOWN BY CLASS
1989 - 90

Class	Number of Students (Frequency)	Percentage (Relative Frequency)
Freshman	4,550	27.7
Sophomore	4,000	24.3
Junior	4,200	25.5
Senior	2,200	13.4
Graduate	1,250	7.6
Other	250	1.5
TOTAL	**16,450**	**100.0**

Charts or graphs are also meaningful data reduction techniques. The two most appropriate charts for qualitative data are the bar chart/graph and the pie chart.

EXAMPLE:

THE NUMBER OF STUDENTS ENROLLED IN XYZ UNIVERSITY BROKEN DOWN BY CLASS 1989 - 90

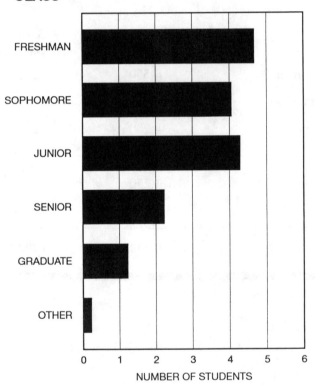

CLASS

VALUES IN THOUSANDS

NOTE: It is also appropriate to present this data in a vertical bar chart.

EXAMPLE:

PIE CHART OF THE NUMBER
OF STUDENTS ENROLLED IN XYZ
UNIVERSITY BROKEN DOWN BY CLASS
1989 - 90

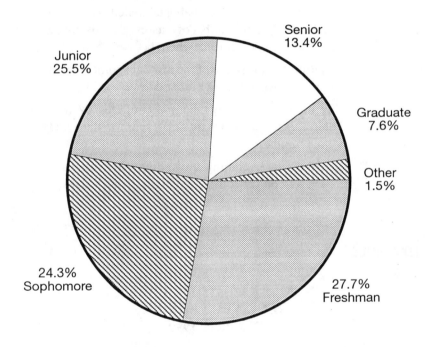

Note that the pie chart expresses the information as a percentage whereas the bar graph typically presents actual count.

b) Quantitative Data

When quantitative data are to be tabulated into frequency distributions, we must determine:

1. The number of non-overlapping classes required for the quantity of data being tabulated;
2. The size of each class (class width); and,
3. The beginning and ending points for each class (class limits).

The steps required include:

1. Finding the first power of 2 that is greater than or equal to the number of data items being tabulated. This power of 2 will be the desired number of classes. Usually, the number of classes needed is somewhere between 5 and 12.
2. Determining the range of the raw data points; i.e., the difference between the highest and lowest values.
3. Dividing the range by the number of classes in order to determine the class size (width) – round to the next largest whole number.
4. Deciding the beginning and ending values for each class depending on the lowest and highest data values.

EXAMPLE:

NUMBER OF PHONE CALLS
RECEIVED PER DAY
IN APRIL 1990

39	42	30	48	35	40
27	25	28	34	33	38
25	34	32	28	42	35
34	37	40	30	31	36
40	45	36	41	34	29

Step 1. Number of classes:

$$2^1 = 2 \qquad 2^4 = 16$$
$$2^2 = 4 \qquad 2^5 = 32*$$
$$2^3 = 8 \qquad 2^6 = 64$$

Step 2. Range = 48 − 25 = 23

Step 3. 23 ÷ 5 = 4.6 or 5 classes

Step 4.

Number of Phone Calls		Number of Days	Percentage of Days
Classes	Tally	Frequency	Percentage
25–29	⦀⦀ I	6	20.0
30–34	⦀⦀ IIII	9	30.0
35–39	⦀⦀ II	7	23.3
40–44	⦀⦀ I	6	20.0
45–49	II	2	6.7
TOTAL		**30**	**100.0**

The most common chart or graph for depicting quantitative frequency distributions is a type of bar chart, known as the **Histogram**.

EXAMPLE:

HISTOGRAM
OF THE NUMBER OF
PHONE CALLS RECEIVED
PER DAY DURING APRIL
1990

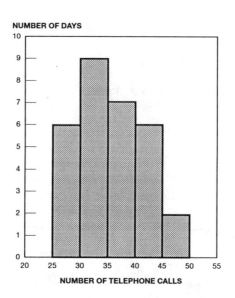

2.2 MEASURES OF
CENTRAL TENDENCY

Measures of central tendency are ways of finding a data value that is central to all the other data values.

a) Arithmetic Mean

The **arithmetic mean** (usually referred to as simply the "mean") is calculated by summing all data values and dividing by the number of data summed.

The formula is:

$$\mu = \frac{\Sigma X}{N}$$

where:

μ = notation for the population mean

Σ = (sigma) = sum of

X = data values

N = number of items in population

or:

$$\overline{X} = \frac{\Sigma X}{n}$$

where:

$\overline{X}$ = the notation for the sample mean

X = data values

n = number of items in sample

EXAMPLE:

Assume the 30 phone calls made in April from the previous example represent sample data. Then,

$$\overline{X} = \frac{1048}{30} = 34.93 \text{ phone calls per day.}$$

b) Weighted Mean

The **weighted mean** is used to average data when all data values do not count (weigh) equally.

The formula is:

$$\overline{X}_w = \frac{\Sigma\,wx}{\Sigma w}$$

where W = Weight assigned to each data value.

EXAMPLE:

Four exams are given during a semester. The grades made by a student along with the assigned weights are shown below.

Grade (X)	% Weight (W)	WX
86	50	4300
75	30	2250
60	10	600
90	10	900
	100	8050

$$\overline{X}_w = \frac{8050}{100} = 80.5 \text{ average grade for course}$$

c) Median

The **median,** symbolized by Md, is the middle value in an array (ordered either from smallest to largest or vice versa) of data. When there is an odd number of observations, the median is equal to the central value in the array; when there is an even number of observations, the two middle values in the array are averaged to determine the median.

EXAMPLE:

ARRAY OF NUMBER
OF PHONE CALLS
RECEIVED PER DAY
IN APRIL
1990

25	29	33	35	38	41
25	30	34	35	39	42
27	30	34	36	40	42
28	31	34	36	40	45
28	32	34	37	40	48

$$Mo = \frac{34 + 35}{2} = 34.5 \text{ phone calls per day}$$

d) Mode

The **mode**, symbolized by Mo, is the value that occurs most often. It is possible for a set of data to have two modes (bimodal) or more (multimodal).

EXAMPLE:

NUMBER OF PHONE CALLS
RECEIVED PER DAY
DURING APRIL 1990

$Mo = 34$ phone calls per day,
because the value 34 occurs four times.

2.3 MEASURES OF VARIATION/ DISPERSION

A measure of variation or dispersion is an indication of the amount of spread or scatter in a data set. One of the purposes of this type of measure is to assess how well an average represents a set of data.

a) Range

The **range**, symbolized by R, is an indication of how much difference exists from the lowest value to the highest value in a set of data.

EXAMPLE:

NUMBER OF PHONE CALLS RECEIVED PER DAY DURING APRIL 1990

$R = 48 - 25 = 23$ phone calls per day.

b) Average Deviation

The **average deviation** measures the average absolute difference between the data values and either the mean or the median.

Method 1. Average Deviation from the Mean
The formula is:

$$AD = \frac{\Sigma |x - \bar{x}|}{n}$$

where: | | is absolute value and indicates that the difference is taken between the data value (x) and the mean $\bar{x}$, but the sign of the difference is ignored.

EXAMPLE:

A sample of 5 days is selected from the 30 days in April, 1990 and the following number of calls were received:

x	$\lvert x - \overline{x} \rvert$
32	5.2
31	6.2
34	3.2
41	3.8
48	10.8
186	29.2

$$X = \frac{\Sigma x}{n} = \frac{185}{5} = 37.2;$$

$$AD = \frac{\Sigma \lvert x - \overline{x} \rvert}{n} = \frac{29.2}{5} = 5.84 \text{ phone calls per day.}$$

Method 2. Average Deviation From the Median

The formula is:

$$AD = \frac{\Sigma \lvert x - Md \rvert}{n}$$

EXAMPLE:

32	2
31	3
34	0
41	7
48	14
	26

Md = 34 (middle observation in array)

$$AD = \frac{\Sigma|x - Md|}{n} = \frac{26}{5} = 5.2 \text{ phone calls per day}$$

c) Standard Deviation

The **standard deviation** is the square root of the average squared deviation between the data values and the mean. It may be calculated for either a sample or a population and the formula notation changes accordingly.

The formulae are:

Population Standard Deviation

$$\sigma = \sqrt{\frac{\Sigma(x - \mu)^2}{N}}$$

Where: σ = (sigma) = symbol for population standard deviation.

or:

Sample Standard Deviation

$$S = \sqrt{\frac{\Sigma(x - \bar{x})^2}{n-1}}$$

where: S = symbol for sample standard deviation.

EXAMPLE:

SAMPLE OF
5 DAYS SELECTED FROM
PHONE CALLS RECEIVED IN APRIL
1990

x	(x-x̄)	(x-x̄)²
32	- 5.2	27.04
31	- 6.2	38.44
34	- 3.2	10.24
41	3.8	14.44
48	10.8	116.64
186	**0**	**206.80**

$$\bar{x} = \frac{186}{5} = 37.2 \quad S = \sqrt{\frac{\Sigma(x-\bar{x})^2}{n-1}} = \sqrt{\frac{206.8}{4}} = \sqrt{51.70}$$

= 7.19 phone calls per day.

NOTE: We assumed in this example that an estimate of the population standard deviation was desired; therefore we used the above equation to calculate S.

d) Variance

The **variance** is the average of the squared deviations between the data values and the mean. (It is the standard deviation squared.) It may also be calculated for either a population or a sample.

The formulae are:

Population Variance

$$\sigma^2 = \frac{\Sigma(x-\mu)^2}{N}$$

Sample Variance

$$S^2 = \frac{\Sigma(x-\bar{x})^2}{n}$$

EXAMPLE:

SAMPLE OF FIVE DAYS OF
PHONE CALLS RECEIVED
DURING APRIL 1990

$S^2 = 51.70^*$ squared phone calls per day.
* This is the value found under the square root sign
from the previous example.

Note that the variance yields an answer in "squared" units; there-fore, its meaning is less readily interpretative for practical application than is the standard deviation. For this reason the standard deviation is typically used in place of the variance as a measure of dispersion.

e) Coefficient of Variation

The **coefficient of variation** is the percentage that the standard deviation of a set of data is of the mean of that same set of data. It is useful when attempting to assess the amount of variation actually represented by the value of a standard deviation. It is also useful when comparing the dispersion across data sets because it reduces all standard deviations from their original units of measure to a percentage.

The formula is:

$$V = \frac{S}{\bar{x}} \times 100$$

EXAMPLE:

SAMPLE OF 5 DAYS OF
PHONE CALLS RECEIVED
DURING APRIL 1990

$$\bar{x} = 37.2 \qquad S = 7.19$$

$$V = \frac{7.19}{37.2} \times 100 = 19.33\%$$

2.4 COMPARISON OF MEASURES

a) Averages

The arithmetic mean $(\bar{x})$ is the most commonly used, and usually the best measure of central tendency. Its calculation involves every data point; therefore, every value in the data set has some influence on the answer. Extreme values, however, may have such an influence on the mean that it fails to be representative. The weighted mean $(\bar{x}_w)$ is a special case of the arithmetic mean. The difference between the two is that the arithmetic mean assumes that every data point weighs equally in the calculation while the weighted mean allows for assigning of weights to the data points based on some preconceived plan.

The median (Md) is a positional measure of central tendency and its value is influenced only by the value of the central observations; extreme values do not greatly influence the value of the median. Therefore, when extreme values are evident, the median generally yields a more representative measure than does the mean.

The mode (Mo) assumes that the value that occurs more frequently than any other value is the most typical. The mode has limited use, but it can be meaningful, especially for qualitative data. Many times a data set will not contain any repeated values; therefore, in those cases, no mode exists.

b) Variation/Dispersion

The range (R) considers only the extreme values within a data set. The average deviation (AD), although it includes every observation within a data set, is not used very frequently. The standard deviation (σ or s) is the most commonly used measure of dispersion, primarily because of theoretical and mathematical reasons beyond the scope of this discussion. The variance (σ^2 or s^2) is the standard deviation squared. The coefficient of variation (V) is a relative measure of variation which allows for a better understanding of the magnitude of the standard deviation.

CHAPTER 3

INTRODUCTION TO PROBABILITY

3.1 WHAT IS PROBABILITY?

Probability is defined as the likelihood of the occurrence of an event or as the chance that some particular event will occur.

EXAMPLE:

A weather report might indicate the chance of rain to be 70% which could be interpreted as the probability of rain = .70.

a) Objective Probability (Calculated)

In most instances, the probability that an event will occur is determined by a mathematical formula and is based on empirical evidence.

$$P(X) = \frac{\text{No. of outcomes corresponding to event } X}{\text{Total no. of possible outcomes}}$$

EXAMPLE:

The probability of drawing a queen from a deck of cards is defined as:

$$P(\text{Queen}) = \frac{\text{No. of queens in the deck}}{\text{Total no. of cards in the deck}} = \frac{4}{52} = \frac{1}{13} \text{ or } .077.$$

b) Subjective Probability

When the probability of an event occurring is based on the personal (or professional) judgment of an individual or group of individuals, the probability is referred to as "subjective."

EXAMPLE:

The probability that sales will increase by $500,000 next year if we increase our advertising expenditure by $10,000 is .25.

3.2   PROPERTIES OF PROBABILITIES

The following three properties are characteristics of all probabilities:

1. $0 \le P(X) \le 1$; every probability is contained within the range 0 to 1, inclusive, where 0 represents absolute certainty that the event will not occur and 1 represents absolute certainty that the event will occur.

EXAMPLE:

P (Head on Coin) $= 1/2$
P (6 on Die) $= 1/6$
P (Ace of Spades) $= 1/52$

2. $\displaystyle\sum_{i=1}^{n} P_i(X) = 1$; the probabilities of all possible simple events

that can occur within a given experiment will sum to 1.

EXAMPLE:

coin: $P(\text{Head}) + P(\text{Tail}) = 1/2 + 1/2 = 1$

die: $P(1) + P(2) + P(3) + P(4) + P(5) + P(6) = 1/6 + 1/6 + 1/6 + 1/6 + 1/6 + 1/6 = 1$

cards: $P(\text{Club}) + P(\text{Heart}) + P(\text{Spade}) + P(\text{Diamond}) = 1/4 + 1/4 + 1/4 + 1/4 = 1$

3. $P(X) + P(\text{Not } X) = 1$; the probability that event X occurs plus the probability that event X does not occur sums to 1.

EXAMPLE:

coin: $P(\text{Head}) + P(\text{Not a Head}) = 1/2 + 1/2 = 1$

die: $P(6) + P(\text{Not a } 6) = 1/6 + 5/6 = 1$

cards: $P(\text{Spade}) + P(\text{Not a Spade}) = 1/4 + 3/4 = 1$ or

$13/52 + 39/52 = 1$

3.3 METHODS OF COMPUTING PROBABILITIES

a) **Addition**

1. Mutually Exclusive Events - those which cannot occur simultaneously. In order to determine the probability that either event X occurs or event Y occurs, the individual probabilities of event X and event Y are added.

$$P(X \text{ or } Y) = P(X) + P(Y)$$

EXAMPLE:

The probability that either a club or a spade is drawn from a deck of cards in a single draw is defined as:

P (Club or Spade) $= P$ (Club) $+ P$ (Spade)

$= 13/52 + 13/52$

$= 26/52$

$= 1/2$ or $.5$

Note: That this concept applies to three or more events as well.

2. Non-Mutually Exclusive Events - those which can occur simultaneously. In order to determine the probability that either event X occurs or event Y occurs, the individual probabilities of event X and event Y are added and the probability that the two occur simultaneously is subtracted from the total.

$$P(X \text{ or } Y) = P(X) = P(Y) - P(X \& Y)$$

EXAMPLE:

The probability that either a Queen or a Spade is drawn from a deck of cards in a single draw is defined as:

P (Queen or Spade) $= P$ (Queen) $+ P$ (Spade) $- P$ (Queen & Spade)

$= 4/52 + 13/52 - 1/52$

$= 16/52$

$= 4/13.$

Notice in this example that we must subtract 1/52 from the total since the Queen of Spades is counted in the total number of Queens and it is also counted in the total number of Spades. If we do not subtract P(Queen & Spade), we are counting that one card twice.

b) Multiplication

1. Independent Events

   Two (or more) events are **independent** if the occurrence of one event has **no effect** upon whether or not the other event occurs. In order to determine the probability that event X occurs and event Y occurs, the individual probability of event X and event Y are multiplied together.

$$P(X \text{ and } Y) = P(X) \times P(Y)$$

EXAMPLE:

1. The probability of tossing a 6 on a single die followed by the toss of a 3 is:

$$
\begin{aligned}
P(6 \text{ and } 3) \quad &= P(6) \times P(3) \\
&= 1/6 \times 1/6 \\
&= 1/36.
\end{aligned}
$$

2. The probability of tossing three heads in 3 tosses of a coin:

$$
\begin{aligned}
P(H, H, H) \quad &= P(H) \times P(H) \times P(H) \\
&= 1/2 \times 1/2 \times 1/2 \\
&= 1/8.
\end{aligned}
$$

3. The probability of drawing a heart from a deck of cards, replacing the first card, and drawing a club on the second draw:

$$
\begin{aligned}
P(H \text{ and } C) \quad &= P(H) \times P(C) \\
&= 13/52 \times 13/52 \\
&= 1/4 \times 1/4 \\
&= 1/16.
\end{aligned}
$$

2. Dependent Events

Two (or more) events are **dependent** if the occurrence of one event has **some effect** upon whether or not the other event occurs. In order to determine the probability that event X occurs and event Y occurs, when X and Y are dependent, the formula is:

$$P(X \text{ and } Y) = P(X) \times P(Y \mid X)$$

or

$$P(X \text{ and } Y) = P(Y) \times P(X \mid Y)$$

where: $P(Y \mid X)$ is read as the probability that event Y will occur, given that event X has already occurred.

And: $P(X \mid Y)$ is read as the probability that event X will occur given that event Y has already occurred.

EXAMPLE:

1. A box contains 6 red balls, 4 green balls, and 5 purple balls. What is the probability that a red ball is drawn on the first draw and a purple ball is drawn on the second draw, if the first ball is **not** replaced prior to the second ball being drawn

$$
\begin{aligned}
P \text{ (Red and Purple)} \quad &= P(R) \times P(P \mid R) \\
&= 6/15 \times 5/14 \\
&= 30/210 \\
&= 1/7
\end{aligned}
$$

2. Three cards are drawn from a deck. What is the probability that the first is a Queen, the second is a Queen, and the third is a King? Assume that each card is **not** replaced prior to the next one being drawn.

$$
\begin{aligned}
P\,(Q1, Q2, K) \quad &= P\,(Q1) \times P\,(Q2|Q1) \times P\,(K|Q1 \,\&\, Q2) \\
&= 4/52 \times 3/51 \times 4/50 \\
&= 48/132{,}600 \\
&= .0004
\end{aligned}
$$

3.4 BAYESIAN DECISION ANALYSIS

Sometimes the probability of an event occurring is influenced by the occurrence of a previous event. When this occurs, the probability is referred to as a conditional probability. Conditional probability is denoted by $P\,(X\,|\,Y)$ and is read as "the probability of event X occurring given that event Y has already occurred." $P\,(X\,|\,Y)$ may be calculated using the following formula:

$$
P(X\,|\,Y) = \frac{P(X\ and\ Y)}{P(Y)}
$$

This formula is frequently "broken down" further and written this way:

$$
P(Y\,|\,X) = \frac{P(X) \times P(Y\,|\,X)}{P(X) \times P(Y\,|\,X) + P(Not\ X)\,P(Y\,|\,Not\ X)}
$$

This latter version is called **Bayes Theorem** and the use of it is called Bayesian Analysis.

EXAMPLE:

Two workers assemble parts from a production process. The probability that worker A makes a mistake in assembling a part is .02 and the probability that worker B makes a mistake is .03. However, worker A assembles 55% of the parts while worker B assembles the remaining 45%. If an assembled part is randomly selected from all of those produced during a given time period and it is determined to be defective, what is the probability that worker A assembled this part?

$$\text{Let } A = \text{Assembled by worker } A$$
$$B = \text{Assembled by worker } B$$
$$(\text{Same as "not } A\text{"})$$
$$D = \text{Defective}$$

$$P(A \mid D) =$$

$$\frac{P(A)\, P(D \mid A)}{P(A) \times P(D \mid A) + P(B) \times P(D \mid B)} =$$

$$\frac{.55 \times .02}{(.55)(.02) + (.45)(.03)} = \frac{.011}{.025} = .449$$

3.5 PROBABILITY TABLES

A tabular approach is often easier to understand when calculating probabilities.

EXAMPLE:

For the previous example, the probability table looks as follows:

ASSEMBLED PARTS

		GOOD	DEFECTIVE	TOTAL
Worker	A	.5390	.0110	.55
	B	.4365	.0135	.45
TOTAL		.9755	.0245	1.00

The **cell** probabilities are referred to as **joint probabilities** which represent the combined probability of the two events (row and column) occurring; e.g., the probability that worker A assembled the part and it is good is .539. The **total** row and column probabilities are referred to as **marginal probabilities** which are the sums of the joint probabilities over the rows or columns. For example, .45 is a marginal probability representing the probability that worker B assembled the part. It is the sum of .4365(probability that worker B assembled it and it is good) plus .0135 (the probability that B assembled it and it is defective).

3.6 PROBABILITY TREE DIAGRAMS

A probability tree diagram is a pictorial approach to solving probability problems where the branches of the tree represent the possible events associated with a given experiment.

EXAMPLE:

For the previous example, the probability tree looks as follows, with G representing a good part.

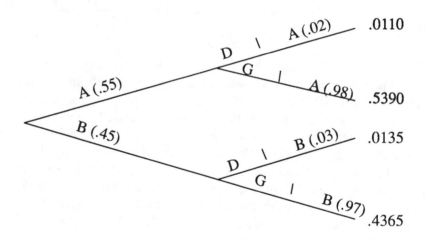

CHAPTER 4

PROBABILITY DISTRIBUTIONS

4.1 RANDOM VARIABLES

The term **random variable** describes the assignment of numerical values to the possible outcomes or events that may occur within a given experiment. For example, if an experiment involves tossing a coin, the random variable could be "number of heads turning up," or if an experiment involves drawing from a deck of cards, the random variable might be "number of red cards drawn," or "number of spades drawn," etc. The term **variable** is used to imply that the number of possible outcomes may "vary," and the term **random** to reflect the idea that the outcome cannot be predicted with absolute certainty.

4.2 DISCRETE PROBABILITY DISTRIBUTIONS

When a random variable can have only certain values within an identified range of values (usually only whole numbers), it is referred to as discrete. Examples of discrete random variables are: number of heads in 5 tosses of a coin, number of spades in 10 cards drawn from an ordinary deck of playing cards, number of 6's tossed on 3 rolls of a die, etc. The term **probability distribution** refers to a representation of all possible values of a random variable together with their associated probabilities.

31

a) Uniform Distribution

A **uniform distribution** is one in which the probability of occurrence of each value of the random variable is the same.

EXAMPLE:

1.   If a single die is rolled, the resulting probability distribution is uniform; i.e.,

$$P(1) = 1/6, P(2) = 1/6, P(3) = 1/6..., P(6) = 1/6.$$

2.   If a coin is tossed, the resulting probability distribution is uniform; i.e.,

$$P(\text{Head}) = 1/2, P(\text{Tail}) = 1/2.$$

3.   If a box contains 5 red balls, 5 white balls, and 5 green balls, the probability distribution is uniform for each color; i.e.,

$$P(\text{Red}) = 1/3, P(\text{White}) = 1/3, P(\text{Green}) = 1/3.$$

b) Binomial Distribution

The **binomial distribution** is characterized by the following three properties:

1.   Each "trial" has exactly **two** possible outcomes, e.g. male or female, yes or no, success or failure, good or defective. This is called the Bernoulli process.

2.   The probability of each outcome remains constant from trial to trial; i.e., the events are independent of each other.

3.   All possible arrangements in which the given event may occur are taken into account when applying the binomial formula.

$$P(X|n, p) = \frac{n!}{x!(n-x)!} p^x q^{n-x}$$

where: x = some value of the random variable

  n = number of trials

  p = constant probability that the event will occur on each trial

  q = 1-p; i.e., the probability that the event will not occur

  ! = factorial; e.g., $5! = 5 \times 4 \times 3 \times 2 \times 1 = 120$.

EXAMPLE:

1. A fair coin is tossed 4 times (or 4 coins are tossed simultaneously). What is the probability that exactly 3 heads will turn up (as opposed to 3 or more)?

$$P\,(x = 3 | n = 4,\, p = 1/2) = \frac{4!}{3!(\,4 - 3\,)!}\,(1/2)^3\,(1/2)^1$$
$$= 4\,(\,1/8\,)\,(\,1/2\,)$$
$$= 4/16$$
$$= 1/4$$

2. Assume that 10% of the items manufactured using a particular process are defective. If 10 items are selected at random from those produced on a given day, what is the probability that only 1 will be defective?

$$P\,(x = 1 | n = 10,\, p = .1\,) = \frac{10!}{1!(\,10{-}1\,)!}\,(\,.10\,)^1\,(\,.90\,)^9$$
$$= .3874$$

3. Compute the probability distribution which represents the tossing of a 6 on a single fair die if the die is tossed 4 times.

  Since a probability distribution is a representation of **all** the possible outcomes associated with a particular experiment, this example will require calculating:

33

$$P(x = 0 | n = 4, p = 1/6) = \frac{4!(1/6)^0(5/6)^4}{0!4!} = .4823$$

$$P(x = 1 | n = 4, p = 1/6) = \frac{4!(1/6)^1(5/6)^3}{1!3!} = .3858$$

$$P(x = 2 | n = 4, p = 1/6) = \frac{4!(1/6)^2(5/6)^2}{2!2!} = .1157$$

$$P(x = 3 | n = 4, p = 1/6) = \frac{4!(1/6)^3(5/6)^1}{3!1!} = .0154$$

$$P(x = 4 | n = 4, p = 1/6) = \frac{4!(1/6)^4(5/6)^0}{4!0!} = .0008$$

Note that the sum of these probabilities is 1, which illustrates Property #2 as outlined in Chapter 3.

c) Hypergeometric Distribution

The **hypergeometric distribution** differs from the binomial distribution in only one characteristic. Whereas in the binomial distribution the probability of occurrence of a particular event remains constant, in the hypergeometric distribution, the probabilities do not remain constant over all possible trials.

$$P(X) = \frac{{}_aC_x\,{}_bC_{n-x}}{{}_NC_n} \text{ , i.e.,}$$

$$P(X) = \frac{\dfrac{a!}{x!(a-x)!}\dfrac{b!}{(n-x)![b-(n-x)!]}}{\dfrac{N!}{n!(N-n)!}}$$

where: x = some value of the random variable
a = number of items in the group having the "success-ful" characteristic
b = number of other items in the group
N = a+b or the total number of items in the group
n = number of trials or number removed from the group
C = combination, e.g., $_aC_x$ = the number of combinations of x items taken from a group of **a** items.

EXAMPLE:

Assume a bag contains 3 red balls, 4 black balls, and 3 green balls. If 4 balls are selected at random and not replaced after each draw, what is the probability that 2 will be red?

$$P(X = 2) = \frac{_3C_2 \,_7C_2}{_{10}C_4}$$

$$= \frac{\dfrac{3!}{2!1!} \dfrac{7!}{2!5!}}{\dfrac{10!}{4!\,6!}}$$

$$= \frac{3 \times 21}{210}$$

$$= \frac{63}{210}$$

$$= .3$$

d) Poisson Distribution

The **Poisson distribution** is used to calculate the probability of occurrence within a time interval or space; e.g., the probability of receiving X phone calls within an hour or the probability that a yard of fabric will contain X number of defects.

$$P(X) = \frac{\mu^x e^{-\mu}}{x!}$$

where: x = some value of the random variable

μ = the average value of the random variable per time period or space

e = a constant 2.718282 which is the base of the natural logarithm.

EXAMPLE:

1. Assume that a company receives an average of 5 phone calls per hour. What is the probability that in a randomly selected hour, the company will receive 7 phone calls?

$$P(x=7) = \frac{5^7 e^{-5}}{7!}$$

$$= \frac{5^7 (2.718282)^{-5}}{7!}$$

$$= \frac{78125 (.006737944)}{5040}$$

$$= .1044$$

2. If a fabric manufacturing process produces an average of 2 defects per yard, what is the probability that a randomly chosen yard of fabric contains 0 defects?

$$P(x = 0) \qquad = \frac{2^0\, e^{-2}}{0!}$$

$$= \frac{2^0 (2.718282)^{-2}}{0!}$$

$$= .1353$$

Note that the mean of the Poisson distribution changes proportionally per time interval or space; e.g., if the mean number of phone calls per hour is 5, the mean number for a 2 hour interval is 10.

The Poisson distribution may also be used to approximate the binomial distribution under certain conditions. When the mean ($\mu = np$) of the binomial distribution is < 10 and n > 20, the Poisson equation is much easier to apply and yields a close approximation to the probability calculated from the binomial formula.

EXAMPLE:

Suppose that 5% of all cars produced by General Motors have some minor defect in the electrical system. If 50 cars are produced in one day, what is the probability that exactly 1 has this minor defect?

Approach 1 - Binomial:

$$P(x{=}1|n{=}50,\, p{=}.05) \;=\; \frac{50!\,(.05)^1\,(.95)^{49}}{1!\,49!}$$

$$= .2025$$

Approach 2 - Poisson (approximate):

$$\mu = np \qquad P(x = 1) = \frac{2.5^1 \, e^{-2.5}}{1!}$$

$$= 50 \,(.05)$$

$$= 2.5 \qquad = \frac{2.5^1 (2.718282)^{-2.5}}{1!}$$

$$= .2052$$

4.3 CONTINUOUS PROBABILITY DISTRIBUTIONS

When a random variable can take on **any** value within a specified range, it is referred to as continuous. Examples of continuous random variables are weight, height, and time.

a) Normal Distribution

The **normal distribution** is the most important of the continuous distributions and is the basis of the majority of the inferential techniques applied in this book. The properties of the normal distribution depicted below are:

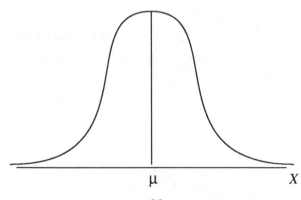

1. The total area under the curve is 1.0; each half = .5.

2. The mean (μ) is located at the center of the distribution.

3. The normal distribution is infinite; theoretically it extends indefinitely in both directions; i.e. it is asymptotic to the x-axis (approaches it, but does not touch it).

4. The Y-axis represents relative frequency. There are greater relative frequencies near the mean and smaller relative frequencies at the extremes. This gives the normal curve its "bell-shaped" appearance.

5. Data that follow any normal distribution can be standardized using:

$$Z = \frac{X - \mu}{\sigma}$$

   where: Z = standard normal score
            X = some value of the random variable
            μ = mean
            σ = standard deviation.

6. Once standardized, areas under any normal curve (probabilities) can be determined from a table of areas under the standard normal curve (these are printed in statistics textbooks, usually in an appendix).

7. The standard normal distribution always has $\mu = 0$ and $\sigma = 1$.

8. Three commonly used areas under the standard normal distribution are:

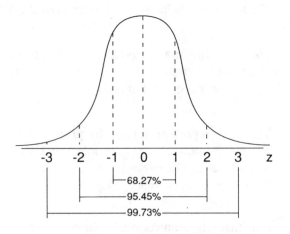

EXAMPLE:

Suppose that the times to complete a given task performed by 1000 individuals normally are distributed and that $\mu = 10.5$ minutes with $\sigma = 2$ minutes.

a) If an individual is selected at random, what is the probability that it will take him between 9 minutes and 11 minutes to complete the task?

STEPS IN SOLVING:

1. Sketch curve to illustrate original distribution.

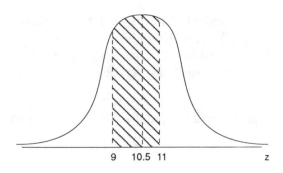

2. Convert to standard normal:

$$Z = \frac{x-\mu}{\sigma} = \frac{9-10.5}{2} = -.75$$

$$Z = \frac{x-\mu}{\sigma} = \frac{11-10.5}{2} = .25$$

3. Sketch the standard normal curve:

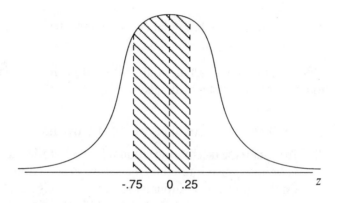

-.75　　0　.25　　　　　　　　　z

4. Refer to Table of Areas under Standard Normal Curve.

If $Z = -.75$*, area from the mean = .2734.
If $Z = .25$, area from the mean = .0987.

* Note that the area for $Z = -.75$ is the same as for $Z = .75$. The negative sign simply indicates that the value is to the left of the mean.

5. As the diagram indicates, since each area is measured from the mean, in order to determine the total shaded area, we must add.

Therefore, the total area under the curve between 9 minutes and 11 minutes ($Z = -.75$ to $Z = .25$) which is also the prob-

41

ability of task completion for an individual randomly selected task is:

.2734 + .0987 = .3721 or approximately 37%.

It is a simple matter to work any problem dealing with areas under the normal curve by sketching the curve and locating the points which define the area(s). Once this is done, observation can dictate whether the areas are to be added or subtracted, or just what manipulation is required.

The normal distribution can also be used to approximate the binomial distribution. The conditions for this approximation are:

1. $n \geq 50$;

2. the mean of the binomial ($\mu = np$) must be > 5; and,

3. $n(1-p)$ must be > 5.

In order to approximate a binomial probability using the normal distribution, the following steps are taken:

1. Verify that the conditions as stated above hold.

2. Adjust for the fact that the binomial, a discrete distribution, is being approximated by a continuous distribution by establishing a range around the value of X (e.g. if we want to know the probability that $X = 20$ in the binomial, we must find the area under the normal curve between 19.5 and 20.5). This adjustment of $\pm.5$ is called a **continuity correction factor.**

3. Calculate Z score(s):

$$Z = \frac{x - \mu}{\sigma}$$

Where: $\mu = np$ and $\sigma = \sqrt{np(1-p)}$, the mean and standard deviation for the binomial distribution.

4. Use the Table of Areas Under the Normal Curve to determine the approximate probability of the event occurring.

CHAPTER 5

SAMPLING AND SAMPLING DISTRIBUTIONS

5.1   TYPES OF SAMPLES

A sample may be selected using either a random selection procedure or a non-random selection procedure. Many times those which are selected randomly are referred to as **probability samples** while those which are selected non-randomly are referred to as **non-probability samples**.

a)   **Non-Probability Samples**

In selecting a non-probability sample, no random or chance selection procedure is applied. A number of selection procedures are available.

Judgment Sample - the selection of sample units is made based on the "judgment" of the one making the selection. Inclusion in the sample is based on the fact that individuals are knowledgeable about the topic being investigated and can, therefore, assist in providing useful information.

Convenience Sample - sampling units are included in the sample because it is "convenient" for them to be included, i.e., they happened to be in the right place at the right time to be selected for inclusion.

Quota Sample - sampling units are included in the sample because they help to meet certain prespecified quotas for the sample.

b) Probability Samples

A probability or random sample is selected in such a way that personal judgment is precluded from the selection process. The most common of these are:

Simple Random Sample - every item in the population has the same chance of selection as any other item in the population and every sample of a given size has the same chance of selection as every other sample of that same size. The statistical methodology covered in this book assumes that samples are selected in this manner.

Systematic Sample - every K^{th} item is selected once a random starting point has been identified. The Kth item is defined by the relationship between the sample size (n) and the popu-lation size (N); i.e., $K = N/n$. The initial random starting point is taken from the first N/n items and may be selected using a table of random numbers.

Stratified Random Sample - the population is divided into homogeneous groups (strata) and a portion of the total sample is selected from each of these strata. The portion of the total sample taken from each stratum depends on the number of items in the strata as well as the degree of variation of the data points within each stratum. Once sampling units are selected and estimates are calculated for each stratum, these results are combined into one overall estimate for the complete population using a weighting scheme. Equations identifying these weighting schemes may be found in higher level statistics texts or in sampling theory textbooks.

Cluster Sample - the population is divided into groups, usually based on geographical regions, e.g., city blocks, districts, counties, and cities. Samples are then selected from a group of randomly selected clusters. The selection process within clusters may involve a census, simple random sampling, or systematic sampling. The overall process may be single staged or multistaged in identifying sampling units for inclusion. The cluster sampling technique is the only one of the four types of probability samples that does not require a complete listing of the elements making up the population.

5.2 RELATIONSHIP BETWEEN SAMPLE DATA AND POPULATION VALUES

A. Definitions

1. **Population** - the total group of objects being studied or investigated.

2. **Sample** - a group of objects that is selected from the population and from which information is gathered.

3. **Statistical Inference** - the methods involved in drawing conclusions about a population based upon information collected from a sample.

B. Sample Information vs. Population Information

Information about a group (population) of objects is often sought. There are basically two ways that people can acquire this information. One is to collect information from every object in the population (a census) and the second is to select a sample from the population and **estimate** the desired information about the population from the sample results. Rarely, if ever, does one collect information from a sample just to study the sample; the ultimate goal is to study the population.

We have previously identified samples as either non probability or probability, depending on the method of selecting the objects to be included in the sample. Only when samples are selected using one of the probability selection techniques does the concept of statistical inference truly apply. In other words, only randomly selected samples allow us to draw accurate conclusions about a population based upon information gathered from a sample. The results from a non-probability or non-random sample may not be extended beyond the actual sample group of subjects. Therefore, care must be taken in designing the sample selection process.

5.3 SAMPLING ERROR

When a sample is selected for an investigation instead of taking a census, it is expected that some difference will exist between the results provided by the sample and the results that would have been provided if a complete census had been taken. This difference is referred to as **sampling error**, and the size of this error will differ from sample to sample. In other words, every sample of a certain size does not yield identical results for a particular estimate, such as the mean. In fact, the results may be substantially different from sample to sample.

If samples are selected using a random technique, the amount of this error can be mathematically calculated, which is another important reason for selecting a probability sampling method, as opposed to one of the non-probability techniques. If we can determine the amount of error that exists in our results, we can also determine the degree of precision or accuracy of the population estimates which are being made from the sample. Sampling error is basically a function of three factors: (1) the size of the sample being used to make the population estimates; (2) the dispersion or scatter of the data points within the population and consequently, the sample, and (3) the degree of confidence one may place on the accuracy of the results.

5.4 SAMPLING DISTRIBUTION OF THE MEAN

If all possible samples of size n are selected from a population of size N, and the mean of some characteristic (e.g., age) is calculated for each sample, these values, along with their respective probability of occurrence, make up the sampling distribution. The number of possible samples of size n that can be drawn from a population of size N is determined using the following formula for a number of combinations:

$$_N C_n = \frac{N!}{n! \ (N-n)!}$$

EXAMPLE:

The number of possible samples of size 10 that can be selected from a population of 100 objects is:

$$_{100} C_{10} = \frac{100!}{10! \ 90!} = 17,310,309,000,000.$$

Note that two samples are different if at least **one** object or value is different.

If it was possible to select every one of these 17,310,309,000,000 samples and calculate the mean age for each, the resulting distribution would be approximately:

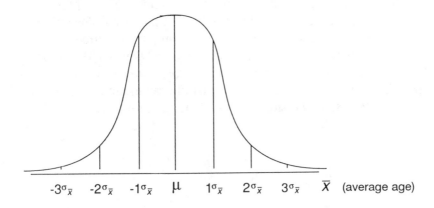

$-3\sigma_{\bar{x}}$ $-2\sigma_{\bar{x}}$ $-1\sigma_{\bar{x}}$ μ $1\sigma_{\bar{x}}$ $2\sigma_{\bar{x}}$ $3\sigma_{\bar{x}}$ $\bar{X}$ (average age)

47

where: $\mu = \dfrac{\Sigma \bar{x}}{_N C_n}$ = The mean of the Sampling Distribution (will be the same as the population mean).

$\sigma_{\bar{x}} = \sqrt{\dfrac{N-n}{N-1}}\ \dfrac{\sigma}{\sqrt{n}}$ = The Standard Error of the Mean (the standard deviation of the sampling distribution).

Note that the above figure looks very much like the normal distribution presented in Chapter 4. It does approach the normal distribution; however, the two are not identical unless the population from which the sample is drawn is normally distributed; i.e., the percentage of areas under the curve between $\pm 1\sigma$, $\pm 2\sigma$, and $\pm 3\sigma$ are not identical to those areas specified by the normal distribution, except in the case of a normally distributed population. More discussion of this will be presented later.

5.5 SAMPLING DISTRIBUTION OF THE PROPORTION

The explanation of the sampling distribution of the proportion parallels that of the sampling distribution of the mean. The only difference is that the distribution consists of sample proportions of some characteristic (e.g., percentage of smokers) and their respective probability of occurrence. The number of possible samples of size n from a population of size N would be calculated in the same manner as discussed earlier. The resulting distribution would look as follows:

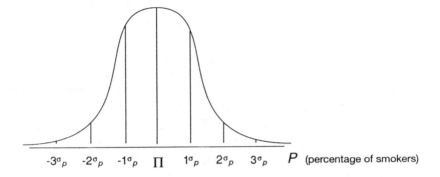

$-3\sigma_p$ $-2\sigma_p$ $-1\sigma_p$ Π $1\sigma_p$ $2\sigma_p$ $3\sigma_p$ P (percentage of smokers)

where: $\Pi = \dfrac{\Sigma p}{{}_N C_n}$ = The mean of the Sampling Distribution (will be the same as the population proportion)

$$\sigma_p = \sqrt{\frac{N-n}{N-1}}\sqrt{\Pi(1-\Pi)/n}$$ = The Standard Error of The Proportion (the standard deviation of the Sampling Distribution).

A similar discussion applies concerning the relationship between this distribution and the normal distribution as that presented for the sampling distribution of the mean.

5.6 THE CENTRAL LIMIT THEOREM

The Central Limit Theorem states:

Regardless of the shape formed by the data values in the population, the shape of the values making up the sampling distribution of the mean ($\overline{X}$'s) will approach a normal distribution having a mean of μ and a standard deviation of $\sigma_{\overline{x}}$ if the sample size is sufficiently large (usually 30 or greater). Likewise, for the sampling distribution of the proportion (p's), if the sample is sufficiently large (usually 50 or greater), this distribution approaches the normal distribution with a mean of Π and a standard deviation of σ_p, when both $n\,\Pi \geq 5$ and $n(1 - \Pi) \geq 5$.

What this theorem is telling us is that if we take sufficiently large samples ($n \geq 30$ for the mean and $n \geq 50$ for the proportion), then we may use normal curve theory in applying statistical inference. That is, if we can assume that our distribution of sample means or sample proportions follows the normal distribution, then we can use the Table of Areas Under the Standard Normal Curve in our applications. The majority of the inferential statistical methods presented in this book make this assumption; i.e., that samples will be large enough to invoke the Central Limit Theorem.

What happens when the sample is not sufficiently large to invoke the Central Limit Theorem? When this is the case, we apply t-distribution theory in our inferential applications when working with the mean. This is many times referred to as small sample theory. The t-distribution will be discussed and applied in Chapters 6 and 7. When we are working with proportions and the sample size is insufficient, the situation calls for the calculation of probabilities and statistical procedures involving the binomial distribution which is beyond the scope of this book. Examples follow illustrating the application of the Central Limit Theorem to practical situations.

EXAMPLE 1: Assume that 1500 students have graduated from the M.B.A. program at XYZ University and their average starting salary is $29,500 with a standard deviation of $2,000. If a sample of 50 students is randomly selected, what is the probability that the average starting salary will be at least $30,000?

SOLUTION: 1. Ascertain that the existing conditions allow for the use of the normal approximation.

Yes, $n \geq 30$.

2. Sketch the distribution of $\overline{X}$'s and locate the area specified.

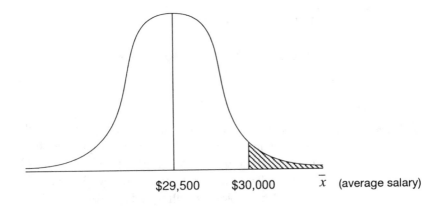

$29,500 $30,000 $\overline{x}$ (average salary)

3. Calculate the Z value.

$$Z = \frac{\overline{x} - \mu}{\sigma_{\overline{x}}}$$

$$= \frac{\overline{x} - \mu}{\sigma / \sqrt{n}}$$

$$= \frac{30,000 - 29,500}{2000 / \sqrt{50}}$$

$$= 1.77$$

4. Determine the area from the mean to $\overline{X} = 30,000$
    ($Z = 1.77$) using the Table of Areas Under the Standard
    Normal Curve.

    If $Z = 1.77$, area = .4616.

5.   Determine the specified probability.

$$P(\overline{X} \geq 30{,}000) = .5 - .4616 = .0384$$

EXAMPLE 2: Assume that the Borg Corporation employs 1600 people, 160 of whom are identified as problem employees due to absenteeism. If a random sample of 100 employees is selected, what is the probability that between 12% and 15% are problem employees with regard to absenteeism?

SOLUTION: 1. Ascertain that the existing conditions allow the use of the normal approximation.

Yes, $n \geq 50$

$$n\,\Pi = 100(.10) = 10$$

$$n\,(1 - \Pi) = 100(.90) = 90.$$

2. Sketch the distribution of p's and locate the area specified.

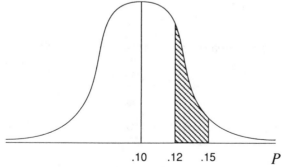

.10   .12   .15 P (% problem employees)

52

3. Calculate Z values.

$$z = \frac{P_1 - \Pi}{s_p} \qquad\qquad z = \frac{P_2 - \Pi}{s_p}$$

$$= \frac{P_1 - \Pi}{\sqrt{\Pi(1-\Pi)/n}} \qquad\qquad = \frac{P_2 - \Pi}{\sqrt{\Pi(1-\Pi)/n}}$$

$$= \frac{.12-.10}{\sqrt{(.10)(.90)/100}} \qquad\qquad = \frac{.15-.10}{\sqrt{(.10)(.90)/100}}$$

$$= .67 \qquad\qquad\qquad = 1.67$$

4. Determine the areas from the mean to $P = .12$ and $P = .15$ using the Table of Areas Under the Normal Curve.

$$\text{If } Z = .67, \text{ area} = .2486.$$
$$\text{If } Z = 1.67, \text{ area} = .4525.$$

5. Determine the specified probability.

$$P(.12 \le p \le .15) = .4525 - .2486$$
$$= .2039.$$

CHAPTER 6

INTERVAL ESTIMATION

6.1 INTERVAL ESTIMATION OF A POPULATION MEAN

In Chapter 5, we discussed the concept of sampling and various methods of sample selection. We noted that the reason we select samples and collect data from sampling units is not so that we can determine something about the sample, but rather, so that we can determine something about the group from which the sample is selected; i.e., the population. It was also discussed that in order for us to project our findings accurately from a sample to the population from which it was drawn, one of the random or probability selection techniques must be used. Also, if the population data are normally distributed and the population standard deviation is known or if the population data are not normally distributed, but the sample size is sufficiently large ($n \geq 30$), the normal distribution may be applied in drawing conclusions about the population, in the second case, due to the Central Limit Theorem.

One of the most common reasons for selecting a sample is to determine the average (mean) of some characteristic within the population. We may, after selecting the sample, calculate the mean of some characteristic and assume that the sample mean is an estimate of the true population mean. When this is done, it is referred to as a **point estimate**. However, if we take the analysis one step further, we may calculate the mean and determine a range about this value within which we can predict that the true population mean is contained, along with the likelihood that this is true. When we do this, we refer to our methodology as an **interval estimate** and calculate it based on normal curve theory if the sample size is sufficient ($n \geq 30$).

A. LARGE SAMPLE ANALYSIS - σ Known

$$Pr\left[\overline{X} - Z\sigma_{\overline{x}} \leq \mu \leq \overline{X} + Z\sigma_{\overline{x}}\right] = \gamma$$

where: $\overline{X}$ =   sample mean

Z =   standard normal score based on Table of Areas Under the Standard Normal Curve

$\sigma_{\overline{x}} = \sigma/\sqrt{n}$ =   standard error of the mean (standard deviation of the sampling distribution)

σ =   population standard deviation

n =   sample size

μ =   population mean (value being estimated)

γ =   probability that the population mean falls within the interval created by the equation.

EXAMPLE:

A service station manager wishes to determine the average number of gallons of gasoline purchased by his customers. He randomly selects 100 customers and determines the average number of gallons purchased by these 100 customers to be 9.5. If it is known that the population standard deviation (σ) of gallons purchased is 2 gallons, calculate a 95% confidence interval estimate for the average number of gallons purchased by the population of customers.

SOLUTION:

1. Specify the values given in the problem:

    n = 100 (size of the sample)

    $\overline{X}$ = 9.5 gals (mean of the sample)

    σ = 2 gals (population standard deviation)

    γ = .95

2. Determine the value of Z for 95% confidence; i.e., determine the standard normal score (Table of Areas Under the Standard Normal Curve) for the sampling distribution of the mean which corresponds to 95% of the area under the curve, symmetrically distributed.

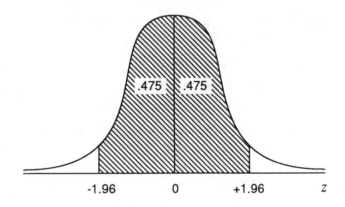

As shown, in this case, Z = ±1.96.

3. Calculate $\sigma_{\overline{x}}$ and substitute known values into the equation for confidence interval calculation.

56

$$\sigma_{\bar{x}} = \frac{\sigma}{\sqrt{n}} \quad \frac{2}{\sqrt{100}} = 2/10 = .2$$

$$Pr\left[\bar{X} - Z\sigma_{\bar{x}} \leq \mu \leq \bar{X} + Z\sigma_{\bar{x}}\right] = \gamma$$

$$Pr\left[9.5 - (1.96)(.2) \leq \mu \leq 9.5 + (1.96)(.2)\right] = .95$$

$$Pr\left(9.5 - .392 \leq \mu \leq 9.5 + .392\right) = .95$$

$$Pr\left(9.108 \leq \mu \leq 9.892\right) = .95$$

4. Interpret the results.

   We can be 95% confident that the average number of gallons of gasoline purchased by all customers is contained within the range of 9.108 gallons to 9.892 gallons, i.e., the estimated population mean is contained between approximately 9.1 and 9.9 gallons, and the likelihood that this is accurate is 95%, as specified in the example.

B. Large Sample Analysis - σ Unknown

In the previous discussion and example, it was assumed that σ, the population standard deviation, was known. This assumption, however, is very unrealistic; i.e., if we are selecting a sample to be used to estimate some average (mean) characteristic in the population, it is not very likely that we would know the value of the population standard deviation. Therefore, it is common practice to substitute the value of the sample standard deviation in place of the population standard deviation. When this is done, the equation for calculating the confidence interval ($n \geq 30$) becomes

$$Pr\left[\overline{X} - Z\hat{\sigma}_{\bar{x}} \le \mu \le \overline{X} + Z\hat{\sigma}_{\overline{X}}\right] = \gamma$$

where: $\quad \hat{\sigma}_{\bar{x}} = \dfrac{S}{\sqrt{n}} \quad$ and $S = \sqrt{\Sigma(x-\bar{x})^2/(n-1)}$.

(Note that in this case, the sample standard deviation is being used to estimate the population standard deviation; consequently, the denominator of $(n\text{ -}1)$ is used).

EXAMPLE:

Assume that a random sample of 500 Power Company customers is selected in order to estimate the average monthly power bill paid. The mean of these 500 customers was calculated to be $105 and the standard deviation was calculated to be $45. Calculate a 99% confidence interval estimate for the average monthly power bill paid by the customers of the Power Company.

Solution: 1. Specify the values given in the problem:

$n = 500$

$\bar{x} = \$105$

$s = \$45$

$1 - \gamma = .99$

2. Determine the value of Z for 99% confidence.

58

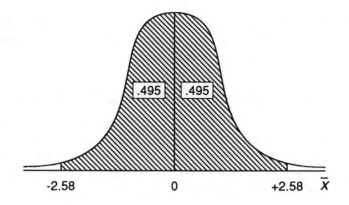

$Z = \pm 2.58$, as shown above.

3. Calculate $\hat{\sigma}_{\bar{x}}$ and substitute values into the confidence interval equation.

$$\hat{\sigma}_{\bar{x}} = \frac{S}{\sqrt{n}} = \frac{\$45}{\sqrt{500}} = 45/22.36 = \$2.01$$

$$Pr\left[\overline{X} - Z\hat{\sigma}_{\bar{x}} \leq \mu \leq \overline{X} + Z\hat{\sigma}_{\bar{x}}\right] = \gamma$$

$$Pr\left[\$105 - (2.58)\,(\$2.01) \leq \mu \leq \$105 + (2.58)\,(\$2.01)\right] = .99$$

$$Pr\left(\$105 - \$5.19 \leq \mu \leq \$105 + \$5.19\right) = .99$$

$$Pr\left(\$99.81 \leq \mu \leq \$110.19\right) = .99$$

4. Interpret the results.

    We can be 99% confident that the average power bill of all the customers of the Power Company is contained within the range of $99.81 to $110.19.

C. Small Sample Analysis -σ Unknown, Normal Population

If the population data follow a normal distribution and the population standard deviation is known, statistical inference procedures based on normal curve theory (using the standard normal distribution Z) apply, regardless of the sample size. If, however, a random sample is selected from normally distributed data and the population standard deviation is not known, the exact distribution for applying statistical inference procedures is the Student's t-distribution. However, t is generally used only when samples are small (n < 30) since samples of 30 or more allow for the use of the standard normal distribution when applying inferential procedures.

The Student's t-distribution, i.e.,

$$t = \frac{\overline{X} - \mu}{S / \sqrt{n}}$$

has the same range of values as the standard normal distribution, is bell-shaped, and is symmetrical about the mean of 0. There is not, however, one "standard" t-distribution; the shape of the t-distribution depends on the size of the sample. The sample size minus 1, $(n - 1)$, is referred to as the **degrees of freedom** and is the parameter (the identifying characteristic) of the distribution. Just as there is a Table of Areas Under the Standard Normal Curve, which we applied in earlier examples, there is also a Table of Areas for the Student's t-Distribution. In this table, areas under the curve are determined for values of t as calculated from the above equation along with the number of degrees of freedom $(df = n - 1)$.

The dispersion or scatter in the t-distribution is greater for smaller sample sizes. Therefore, very small samples result in a t-distribution having greater area in the tails and less area in the central portion of the curve. On the other hand, as the sample size becomes larger, this situation reverses so that once the sample size reaches approximately 30, there is very little difference between the shape of the t-distribution and the shape of the standard normal distribution. Thus, there is justification for using the Z statistic for samples of 30 or greater, rather than the t statistic.

EXAMPLE:

Assume that information is desired on the daily average amount of waste dumped at a landfill in a certain county in Florida over the past year.

A random sample of 25 days was selected and information on tons of waste dumped was collected. The mean amount was calculated from the sample to be 110 tons. Since no information existed as to the population standard deviation, the sample standard deviation was also calculated and that value was 25 tons. Also, it is assumed that landfill waste tonnage follows a normal distribution. Construct a 95% confidence interval estimate for the average daily tonnage of landfill waste.

SOLUTION:

1. Identify the appropriate distribution.

   The t distribution is appropriate due to:

   a) normally distributed population

   b) σ unknown

   c) $n < 30$.

2. State known values:

$$n = 25$$
$$\overline{X} = 110 \text{ tons}$$
$$S = 25 \text{ tons}$$
$$\gamma = .95$$

3. Set up equation for confidence interval estimate:

$$Pr\left[\bar{X} - t\hat{\sigma}_{\bar{x}} \leq \mu \leq \bar{X} + t\hat{\sigma}_{\bar{x}}\right] = \gamma$$

where $\hat{\sigma} = S / \sqrt{n}$

4. Determine the value of t from the Student's t-distribution:

$df = n - 1$

$\quad = 25 - 1$

$\quad = 24$

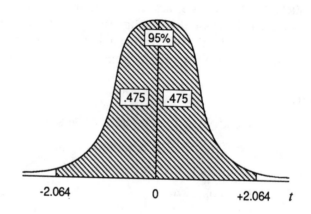

and $t = \pm 2.064$.

5. Substitute values into the confidence interval equation.

$$\hat{\sigma}_{\bar{x}} = S / \sqrt{n}$$
$$= 25 / \sqrt{25}$$
$$= 5$$

$$Pr\left[110 - 2.064(5) \le \mu \le 110 + 2.064(5)\right] = 95\%$$
$$Pr\left(110 - 10.32 \le \mu \le 110 + 10.32\right) = 95\%$$
$$Pr\left(99.68 \le \mu \le 120.32\right) = 95\%$$

6. Interpret the results.

    We can be 95% confident that the average daily land-fill tonnage over the past year is contained within the range of 99.68 tons to 120.32 tons.

6.2 INTERVAL ESTIMATION OF A POPULATION PROPORTION

As we observed in Chapter 5, the sampling distribution of the proportion approaches a normal distribution with a mean of a Π and standard deviation of σ_p if the sample size is 50 or greater, and both $n\Pi$ and $n(1-\Pi)$ are ≥ 5, where:

$$\sigma_p = \sqrt{\Pi(1-\Pi)/n}.$$

Therefore, we may take the same approach for estimating a population proportion as we have just discussed for a population mean. However, the above equation for the standard error of the proportion must be changed to reflect the use of p (sample proportion) rather than Π (the population proportion). After all, it is the value of Π which we are trying to estimate. Therefore, it is obvious that if we desire to estimate this value that it is unknown, we cannot possibly use an equation that requires the substitution of this unknown value. Thus, the equation for a confidence interval estimate for a proportion becomes:

$$ Pr\left[P - Z\hat{\sigma}_p \leq \Pi \leq P + Z\hat{\sigma}_p\right] = \gamma $$

where:

P = sample proportion (point estimate)

Z = standard normal score

$\hat{\sigma}_p = \sqrt{P\,(1-P)/n}$

n = sample size

Π = population proportion being estimated

γ = likelihood that the population proportion will fall within the range established by confidence interval.

EXAMPLE:

A random sample of 100 employees was selected from all of the employees of the Federal Corp. in order to determine the percentage of employees who feel that improvements are needed in the supervisor/worker relationship. Of the 100 surveyed, 67 made this indication. Construct a 90% confidence interval.

SOLUTION: 1. Determine if the normal distribution is appropriate for this problem:

Yes: $n \geq 50$, $n\hat{\Pi} \geq 5$, $n\left(1 - \hat{\Pi}\right) \geq 5$.

2. Specify stated values:

$$n = 100$$
$$\hat{\Pi} = p = .67$$
$$\gamma = .90$$

3. Determine the appropriate value of Z using the Table of Areas Under the Standard Normal Curve.

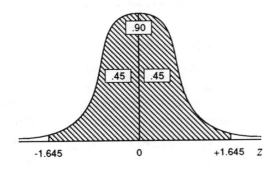

$$Z = \pm 1.645.$$

4. Calculate the confidence interval.

$$\hat{\sigma}_p = \sqrt{P(1-P)/n}$$

$$= \sqrt{(.67)\ (.33)/100}$$

$$= .047.$$

$$Pr\left[.67 - 1.645\,(.047) \leq \prod \leq .67 + 1.645\,(.047)\right] = .90$$

$$Pr\left(.67 - .077 \leq \prod \leq .67 + .077\right) = .90$$

$$Pr\left(.593 \leq \prod \leq .747\right) = .90$$
or

$$Pr\left(59.3\% \leq \prod \leq 74.7\%\right) = .90$$

---

5. Interpret the results.

   We can be 90% confident that the proportion (percentage) of all those employed by the Federal Corp. who believe that improvements are needed in the supervisor/worker relationship is contained within the range of . 593 to .747 (59.3% to 74.7%).

If the sample size is less than 50 when working with inferential procedures involving proportions, the proper distribution is the binomial distribution. These procedures are beyond the scope of this book.

6.3 DETERMINING THE SIZE OF THE SAMPLE

We have previously illustrated a number of examples in which we "assumed" the sample to be a given size. However, in actual practice we do not just "pick" or "assume" a sample size. A number of factors must be taken into consideration and actually the appropriate sample size to use in a particular situation is a value which can be calculated from an equation rather than just picked out of the air. Even though sample size determination is being included as the last topic in this chapter, it is one of the first considerations in statistical estimation. Obviously, we should not begin questioning people or collecting information until we know how many people or objects to include.

a) Sample Size Determination for Estimating a Mean

One of the most common reasons for selecting a sample and collecting information is so that we may use the information to calculate an average (mean) which is used as an estimate of the mean for the entire group of objects; i.e., the population. We have seen that estimates are made either as **point estimates** (the sample mean) or as interval estimates (confidence intervals).

The number of items (n) to be included in a sample (i.e., sample size) is a function of three components:

1. the maximum error desired by the user(s) of the information;

2. the level of confidence desired by the user(s) of the information; and,

3. the degree of variation or dispersion of the data points within the population and consequently the sample.

$$n = \left(Z\sigma/E\right)^2$$

where:

n = sample size

Z = standard normal score from the Table of Areas Under the Standard Normal Curve – based on the degree of confidence specified by the user(s) of the information

σ = population standard deviation

E = maximum error allowed by the user(s) of the information

As indicated above, in order to determine the sample size (n) needed in a given situation, in addition to the information provided by those who plan to use the information, the value of σ, the population standard deviation is required. It is conceivable, although not likely, that this value might be available from some past study or prior knowledge. When the value of σ is not known, it must be estimated by the value from a pilot study, which is a small sample selected for the purpose of estimating a value to be used for σ.

EXAMPLE:

A sample is to be selected from the sales receipts of the Cute Clothing Store so that an estimate can be made as to the average amount spent per purchase at the store within the past month. The store manager wishes the estimate to be made with 95% confidence and specifies that the maximum acceptable error for this estimate should not exceed $5. Assume that a pilot study revealed an estimated population standard deviation to be $25. Calculate the sample size needed for this estimate.

SOLUTION:

1. Specify values given:

σ = $25.00

E =   5.00.

2. Determine value of Z from Table of Areas Under the Normal Curve:

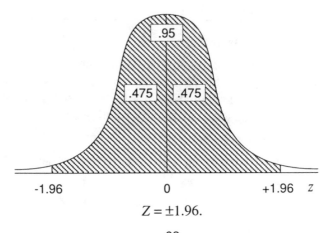

$Z = \pm 1.96.$

68

3. Substitute values into the equation for sample size calculation:

$$n = (Z\,\sigma/E)^2$$
$$= [1.96\,(25)/5]^2$$
$$= 96.04 \text{ or } 97 \text{ customers.}$$

Note that a fractional value is always rounded up to the next largest whole number (integer). Obviously, we cannot select a fractional sampling unit and if we don't round up as opposed to rounding to the nearest whole number, the sample size may be insufficient for the desired precision of the study.

Now let's take this example one step further. As we have said, this is the first step in the estimation process, so let's suppose that we actually take sales receipts for the Cute Clothing Store and randomly select 97 to serve as a sample. We record from these 97 receipts the amounts spent and calculate the mean to be $125 and an estimate of the population standard deviation to be $30. We can then make a 95% confidence interval estimate which the example indicates is the purpose for taking the sample.

$$Pr\left[\$125 - 1.96\left(30/\sqrt{97}\right) \le \mu \le \$125 + 1.96\left(30/\sqrt{97}\right)\right] = .95$$

or

$$Pr\left(\$119.03 \le \mu \le \$130.97\right) = .95.$$

We conclude that we can estimate, with 95% confidence, that the average sale of the Cute Clothing Store is contained within the range of $119.02 to $130.97.   Did we meet the specifications made by the user of the information, who in this case is the store manager? The answer to this question is no. You recall that the manager specified that the maximum error should not exceed $5; i.e., our estimate could be as much as $5 off, either above or below the true value, but no more than $5. The error in this case is:

$$\text{Error} = Z\left(\hat{\sigma}/\sqrt{n}\right)$$

$$= 1.96\left(30/\sqrt{97}\right)$$

$$= \$5.97$$

or

$$\$130.97 - \$125$$

$$= \$5.97.$$

which is $.97 greater than what was allowed. When this occurs, it is an indication that the sample size selected was insufficient (too small) for the desired precision of the estimate. If desired, we could increase the sample by adding additional units to those already selected and reworking the confidence interval. The number of additional units to add may be determined by recalculating n, using the value of s from the sample rather than relying on the value estimated from the pilot study.

$$n = [1.96\,(30)/5]^2$$
$$= 138.3 \text{ or } 139.$$

Therefore, the additional number of units to be selected would be determined by subtracting the original value of 97 from the newly calculated value of 139 to yield an additional 42 sales receipts to be randomly selected from those remaining.

b. Sample Size Determination for Estimating a Proportion

Another common purpose for selecting a sample is to estimate the proportion of some characteristic in the population. Just as there is an equation for determining the sample size to estimate a mean, there is also an equation that allows us to determine the number of units to select for estimating a population proportion. This calculation is also based on the degree of accuracy and level of confidence desired by the user(s) of the information.

$$n = \frac{Z^2 \, \Pi \, (1-\Pi)}{E^2}$$

where:

n = sample size

Z = standard normal score based on the degree of confidence desired by user(s) of the information

Π = population proportion having the characteristic of interest

E = maximum error allowed by the user(s) of the information.

This equation, as it is written, requires the knowledge of Π, the population proportion having the characteristic of interest. It is obvious that if we know the value of Π, then there is no need to take a sample to estimate it. Therefore, rather than substituting the value of Π into the sample size equation, the value to be substituted will be some estimate of the value of Π. As with σ in the formula for sample size calculation for mean estimates, the value used for Π may be from past experience or from a pilot study which is based on a very small sample. We will use the symbol $\hat{\Pi}$ for an estimate of Π.

EXAMPLE:

A local retailer is interested in determining the effectiveness of his newspaper advertisements. He wishes to question his customers with regard to the influence the newspaper ads

71

have on their purchase decisions. How many customers should he question if he desires 99 percent confidence with a maximum error of 5%? Assume that the retailer believes from his own knowledge of prior experience that approximately 75% of all purchases are influenced by his newspaper advertisements.

SOLUTION: 1. Specify values given

$$\hat{\Pi} = .75$$
$$E = .05.$$

2. Determine value of Z from Table of Areas Under the Standard Normal Curve:

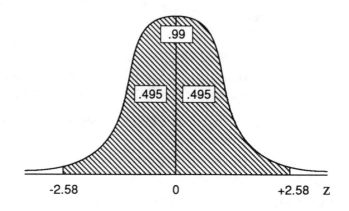

$$Z = \pm 2.58$$

3. Substitute values into the equation for Sample Size Calculation.

$$n = \left[Z^2 \, \hat{\Pi} \left(1 - \hat{\Pi} \right) \right] / E^2$$

$$= \left[2.58^2 \, (.75) \, (.25) / .05^2 \right]$$

$$= 499.22 \text{ or } 500 \text{ customers}$$

72

If no information exists from the past relative to an estimate of the proportion in the population having the characteristic of interest and if there is no time to conduct a pilot study, the calculation of the sample size may be performed by using the value $\hat{\Pi} = .5$. When using $\hat{\Pi} = .5$, obviously $(1 - \hat{\Pi} = .5)$; when this is the case, we will arrive at the maximum or largest sample size that would be needed for the specified degree of confidence and acceptable error. This is due to the fact that $(.5)(.5) = .25$ is the largest possible product of any two numbers which sum to 1. No comparable situation exists, however, when calculating the sample size for the mean estimate. That is, there is no value which we can substitute for σ other than one from prior experience or from a pilot study.

EXAMPLE:

Assume that the same conditions exist as those specified in the previous example; however, assume that there is no knowledge from prior experience as to the possible proportion who are influenced in their purchase decisions by newspaper advertising. What sample size would be required under these conditions?

SOLUTION: 1. Specify given values.

$$E = .05$$
$$\hat{\Pi} = ?$$

2. Determine the value of Z from Table of Areas Under the Standard Normal Curve.

$$Z = \pm 2.58$$

3. Substitute the values into the equation for Sample Size calculation.

$$n = \left[Z^2 \; \hat{\Pi} \left(1-\hat{\Pi}\right)\right]\big/E^2$$

$$= \left[2.58^2 \; (.5) \; (.5)\right]\big/(.05)^2$$

(Note that $\hat{\Pi}$ equals .5 due to
lack of other information.)

$$= 665.64 \; = \; 666 \text{ customers}$$

If we select a random sample of 666 customers, we are assured that our estimate will be made in agreement with the specifications set by the user(s) of the information. There would be no reason to select a larger sample than 666 under these conditions. Note that 666 is larger than 500, the sample size obtained when $\hat{\Pi} = .75$ was used.

CHAPTER 7

HYPOTHESIS TESTING

7.1 REASONS FOR TESTING HYPOTHESES

The Random House Dictionary defines the term **hypothesis** as an unproved or unverified assumption that can be either used or accepted as probable in the light of established facts. This definition applies as well to a statistical interpretation of the term hypothesis. In statistical inference methodology, a hypothesis is a statement of a condition which is assumed to exist in a population and is tested using the results from a randomly selected sample. For example, a candidate for public office assumes that he will receive at least fifty percent of the votes in a particular election; the president of a bank may assume that his average balance per customer is $500; or the production manager of an assembly process may have reason to believe that the process is operating with only a 2% rate of defectives.

These statements or claims should not be used as statements of fact or belief unless there is some evidence of the validity of such statements. Therefore, prior to announcing these types of information either through advertisements or other means, tests should be conducted to determine whether or not the statements should be accepted and with what likelihood of accuracy. We, therefore, randomly select voters, or customer accounts, or assembled items, etc. and use the results from these randomly selected sampling units to test against what is believed to be true in the population. Based on the outcome of the test, action might then be taken, for example, relative to changes in campaign strategy, new marketing strategy allowing incentives for the purpose of increasing customer bank balances, readjusting a machine, or swapping out workers.

Basically, hypothesis testing is performed to investigate preconceived assumptions about some condition in the population. Usually this condition can be expressed as an average of some characteristic or as a percentage of some characteristic of interest. Sample data are selected and either the sample average (mean) or percentage (proportion) is calculated in order to determine if this value could reasonably be assumed to exist within the hypothesized population.

7.2 STEPS IN HYPOTHESIS TESTING

Any hypothesis test, regardless of whether it involves means or proportions, can be solved following a step-by-step approach. The number of steps may vary from textbook to textbook, but the end results will be the same regardless of whether we use five steps, seven steps, or ten steps. Five steps are outlined below for solving hypothesis testing problems.

STEPS IN HYPOTHESIS TESTING

Step 1.   a)   State the null hypothesis (H_0), which is the statement that we test. As the term "null" implies, this is an assumption of "no relationship," or "no difference" concerning the parameter(s) of interest. For example:

H_0: $\mu = C$, $\mu \geq C$, $\mu \leq C$; i.e., the population mean is equal to some prespecified value of C, at least some prespecified value of C, or at most some prespecified value of C.

H_0: $\Pi = C$, $\Pi \geq C$, $\Pi \leq C$; i.e., the population proportion is equal to some prespecified value of C, at least some prespecified value of C, or at most some prespecified value of C.

H_0: $\mu_1 = \mu_2$, $\mu_1 \geq \mu_2$, $\mu_1 \leq \mu_2$; i.e., two population means are identical, or the mean of population 1 is greater than or equal to that of population 2, or the mean of population 1 is less than or equal to that of population 2.

H_0: $\Pi_1 = \Pi_2$, $\Pi_1 \geq \Pi_2$, $\Pi_1 \leq \Pi_2$; i.e., two population proportions are identical, or the proportion in population 1 is greater than or equal to that of population 2, or the proportion in population 1 is less than or equal to that of population 2.

b) State the alternative hypothesis (H_1) which is based on the belief of the investigator relative to the relationship between the parameter(s). Three options are available in basic hypothesis tests:

1. There is a "difference" in values being investigated. For example:

H_1: $\mu \neq C$; i.e., the population mean is not the same as the prespecified value of C.

H_1: $\Pi \neq C$; i.e., the population proportion is not the same as the prespecified value of C.

H_1: $\mu_1 \neq \mu_2$; i.e., the two population means are not the same value.

H_1: $\Pi_1 \neq \Pi_2$; i.e., the two population proportions are not the same value.

2. One value is "greater than" another value. For example:

H_1: $\mu > C$; i.e., the population mean is greater than the prespecified value of C.

H_1: $\Pi > C$; i.e., the population proportion is greater than the prespecified value of C.

H_1: $\mu_1 > \mu_2$; i.e., the mean in population 1 is greater than the mean in population 2.

H_1: $\Pi_1 > \Pi_2$; i.e., the proportion of some characteristic in population 1 is greater than the proportion of the same characteristic in population 2.

3. One value is "less than" another value. For example:

H_1: $\mu < C$; i.e., the population mean is less than the prespecified value of C.

77

$H_1: \Pi < C$; i.e., the population proportion is less than the prespecified value of C.

$H_1: \mu_1 < \mu_2$; i.e., the mean in population 1 is less than the mean in population 2.

$H_1: \Pi_1 < \Pi_2$; i.e., the proportion of some characteristic in population 1 is less than the proportion of the same characteristic in population 2.

Step 2.   Specify the values given in the problem.

Step 3.   Determine the appropriate distribution and a critical value from either:

A.   The Table of Areas Under the Standard Normal Curve (Z); or

B.   The Table of the Student's t-distribution (t), depending on which is appropriate for the particular problem being solved.

Step 4.   Solve for the sample value of Z or t (whichever is appropriate) using the appropriate equation for the value.

Step 5.   Draw a conclusion as to whether H_0 should be rejected or whether we should fail to reject H_0.

Rule A.   If the absolute value of the computed value from Step 4 is greater than or equal to the absolute value of the table value from Step 3, reject the null hypothesis (H_0) and accept the alternative hypothesis (H_1).

Rule B.   If the computed value from Step 4 is less than the absolute value of the table value from Step 3, fail to reject the null hypothesis (H_0) which requires no action to be taken regarding H_1. This is simply an indication that the sample results are sufficient to allow us to reject the null hypothesis (H_0). This could be viewed as a lack of a definitive conclusion.

7.3 HYPOTHESIS TESTS ON MEANS

One of the most common types of hypothesis tests is that dealing with the testing of means. This type of test may deal with testing to determine if a population mean can be concluded to be equal to a pre-specified value. The test may deal with small samples or large samples, and with the population standard deviation (σ) being known or unknown. Also, tests involving means may involve two populations and may be either independent tests or dependent (matched pairs) tests. Two population tests will be covered in the next volume, *The Essentials of Business Statistics II*.

A. Testing Whether the Population Mean Is Equal to a Pre-specified Value – Normally Distributed Population with σ Known.

As we saw in confidence interval estimation in Chapter 6, if the population from which the sample is drawn is normally distributed relative to the variable of interest, and if we know the value of the population standard deviation (σ), regardless of the size of the sample, the standard normal distribution (Z) may be applied in the solution.

EXAMPLE 1:

The manager of Quik Burger believes that his customers travel an average of 5 miles, one way, to dine at his restaurant. In order to test this belief, the manager randomly selects 25 customers one evening and asks each how far they drive from their home to the restaurant. He calculated the mean distance to be 7.5 miles. It is known that distance traveled is normally distributed and the standard deviation (σ) is 4 miles. Test to determine if the manager's belief is accurate. Make this test at a .05 level of significance, which will be denoted by the symbol α.

SOLUTION:

Step 1.   State the null hypothesis and alternative hypothesis.

H_0: μ = 5 miles (assumption to test)

H_1: $\mu \neq 5$ miles (two-tailed test)

Note that we use ≠ in H_1:; this is due to the fact that the problem did not indicate that a direction (either > or <) was of interest. This also means that we will use a two-tailed test, as explained in more detail later.

Step 2.   Specify the values given in the problem.

$\mu = 5$ miles (assumed)

$n = 25$ (size of sample)

$\overline{X} = 7.5$ miles (calculated from the sample of 25 customers)

$\sigma = 4$ miles (known value of the population standard deviation)

$\alpha = .05$ (level of significance).

Step 3.   Determine the appropriate distribution and a critical value from the appropriate table.

In this problem the Z-Table of Areas Under the Standard Normal Curve is appropriate. This is due to the fact that the population of distances traveled is normally distributed and because σ is known as specified in the problem. The size of the sample is not a factor here due to the knowledge of these facts. The table value is determined based on the level of significance, α, specified in the problem. ***Alpha (α) is defined as the probability of rejecting the null hypothesis (H_0) when it is indeed accurate and should not be rejected.*** The table value is, in addition, based on whether we are using a one-tailed or two-tailed test; in this case it is two-tailed since the alternative hypothesis is ≠ and no direction (> or <) was specified in H_1. Anytime the alternative hypothesis (H_1) is ≠, we use the a two-tailed test.

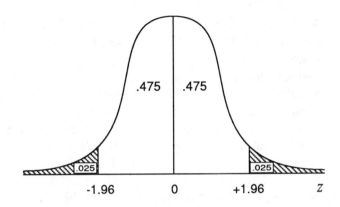

Since $\alpha = .05$ and we are using a two-tailed test, $\frac{1}{2}$ of α will be placed in each tail of the curve. The Table of Areas Under the Standard Normal Curve will then be used to determine the values of Z which correspond to the critical values. Therefore $Z = \pm 1.96$.

Step 4. Solve for the sample value of Z using the following equation:

$$Z = \frac{\overline{X} - \mu}{\sigma/\sqrt{n}}$$

$$= \frac{7.5 - 5}{4/\sqrt{25}}$$

$$= 2.5/.8$$

$$= 3.125.$$

Step 5. Draw a conclusion.

Here, Rule A applies, i.e., the computed value of 3.125 is greater than the table value of 1.96. Therefore, we reject H_0: $\mu = 5$ and accept H_1: $\mu \neq 5$ which means we have a strong (statistically significant) evidence that the belief of the manager is incorrect. Instead, we strongly believe that the average distance traveled to his restaurant from his customers' homes is **not** 5 miles. There is, however, up to a 5% chance that we are in error ($\alpha = .05$ - the probability of rejecting a true null hypothesis). Note that we cannot conclude that the average distance is greater than 5 miles, only that it is not 5 miles. This is due to the way we tested. If we were interested in determining if the average distance were greater than 5 miles, the alternative hypothesis would have been written that way, a one-tailed test would have been used, and the table value determined accordingly would have been different.

Another way of arriving at the same conclusion is by looking at the diagram of the distribution and locating the computed value either in the rejection region, or the fail-to-reject region as illustrated below.

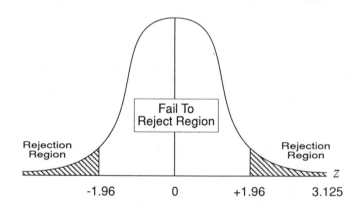

There is less than a 5% probability that we would get an $\overline{X}$-value as large as 7.5 by chance alone, if the hypothesis H_0: $\mu = 5$ is actually true.

Note that 3.125 (the computed value of Z) falls in the rejection region (to the right of $Z = 1.96$) and therefore results in the same conclusion as that from using Rule A. The overall outcome of this test might influence the manager of Quik Burger in his promotion and advertising strategy.

EXAMPLE 2:

The executives of the Skyway Theme Park believe that the average daily amount spent per customer at the park is at least $25, including admission. In order to test this belief, they randomly sample 100 visitors as they exit the park and gather information on expenditures per person. The average amount spent was calculated to be $22.50. The standard deviation of the amounts spent for all visitors (σ) is known to be $12.50. It is known also that the population amounts spent follow a normal distribution. Test at the $\alpha = .05$ level of significance in order to determine if the executives of the Skyway Theme Park are accurate in their belief.

SOLUTION:

Step 1. $H_0: \mu \geq \$25$ (assumption to test)

$H_1: \mu < \$25$ (1-tailed test, because a specific direction (<) is used).

Step 2. $\mu = \geq \$25$ (assumed)

$n = 100$ (number of visitors sampled)

$\overline{X} = \$22.50$ (mean calculated from the 100 visitors)

$\sigma = \$12.50$ (known value of population standard deviation)

$\alpha = .05$ (level of significance).

Step 3. The Z-test is appropriate due to the fact that the amounts spent in the population are normally distributed and σ is known. Whenever the alternative hypothesis (H_1) is > or < (< in this case), we use a one-tailed test. Since the test is one-tailed, the area specified by α (in this example, $\alpha = .05$) is located only in one side (or tail) of the curve as opposed to being split as with the two-tailed test. The appropriate tail of the curve in which to place this value of α is determined by the directional sign in the

83

alternative hypothesis; i.e., if H_1 specifies <, the α value will be placed in the left tail and if H_1 specifies >, the α value will be placed in the right tail of the curve. Therefore, $Z = -1.645$.

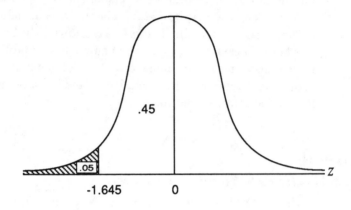

Step 4.

$$Z = \frac{\overline{X} - \mu}{\sigma/\sqrt{n}}$$

$$= \frac{22.50 - 25}{12.5/\sqrt{100}}$$

$$= -2.50/1.25$$

$$= -2.00.$$

Step 5. Since $|-2.00| > 1.645$, Rule A says that we should reject H_0 and accept H_1. This means we have strong evidence that the park executives were incorrect in their belief that the daily average spent per customer was at least \$25. In other words, we conclude, as H_1 states, that the average per person is probably actually less than \$25. However, there is a 5 percent chance that we are in error ($\alpha = .05$ – the probability of rejecting a true null hypothesis).

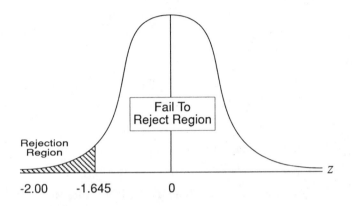

Note that -2.00 falls in the rejection region, an indication that H_0 should be rejected, just as was indicated from Rule A.

B. Testing That the Population Mean Is a Prespecified Value - No Knowledge of the Population Distribution - σ Known or Unknown - Large Sample

We have already seen that if we have no knowledge relative to the shape of the population as well as no knowledge of σ, then the Central Limit Theorem allows for the use of the Z-distribution (standard normal distribution) in statistical inference if the sample size is sufficiently large ($n \geq 30$). This section deals with this specific situation. The steps involved in testing hypotheses under these conditions are the same as those outlined in the previous section.

EXAMPLE 1:

A random sample of 125 days shows that workers on a particular assembly line have produced, on the average, 244 parts per day. The prescribed rate for this production, based on historical data, is 240 parts per day. At the .01 level, do these sample results allow us to conclude that this system is truly producing at a greater rate than what has been done historically? Due to the fact that no information was available as to the value of σ (the population standard deviation), s (the sample standard deviation) was calculated to be 20.5 parts per day.

SOLUTION:

Step 1.

$H_0: \mu = 240$ (assumption to test)

$H_1: \mu > 240$ (1-tailed test).

Step 2. $\mu = 240$ (assumed)

$n = 125$ (number of days sampled)

$\overline{X} = $ parts per day (calculated from sample)

$\sigma = 20.5$ parts per day (calculated from sample)

$\alpha = .01$ (level of significance).

Step 3. The Z test is appropriate due to the sample size being sufficiently large (n ≥ 30) to invoke the Central Limit Theorem. Since we are using a one-tailed test, and H_1 is >, the $\alpha = .01$ will be placed in the right tail of the curve.

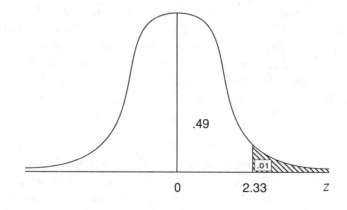

Therefore, $Z = 2.33$.

Step 4.

$$Z = \frac{\overline{X} - \mu}{s / \sqrt{n}}$$

$$= \frac{244 - 240}{20.5 / \sqrt{125}}$$

$$= 4 / 1.834$$

$$= 2.182$$

Step 5.

Since $2.182 < 2.33$, Rule B says that we should fail to reject H_0. This indicates that we do not have strong enough evidence to support the idea that our system is operating at a rate in excess of what has been true historically. We can basically attribute the apparent difference (244 vs. 240) to the fact that 244 was calculated from a sample and that sampling error is, therefore, present. The probability that this conclusion is in error is not based upon α and the calculations required to determine it is beyond the scope of the material in this text. Again, we can show this conclusion with a pictorial approach.

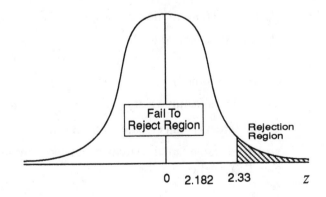

C. Testing That the Population Mean Is a Prespecified Value- Normally Distributed Population - σ Unknown - Small Sample

As we discussed in Chapter 6, if the population from which a sample is selected is normally distributed relative to the characteristic being studied, and if the population standard deviation (σ) is not known and a sample size is less than 30, the exact distribution is the Student's t-distribution. Once the sample is 30 or greater, we typically use the Z-distribution as an approximation to the t-distribution due to the close similarity between the two distributions under this condition. The Student's t-distribution is a function of the number of degrees of freedom which is determined by subtracting 1 from the sample size ($df=n-1$). Again, the same five step outline, as illustrated previously, may be used to solve an hypothesis testing problem using the t-distribution.

EXAMPLE 1:

The manufacturer of rubber hoses produces what is advertised to be a 100-foot hose. In order to test the accuracy of their advertisement, they randomly selected 25 hoses and determined the average length to be 98.9 feet and the standard deviation to be 1.5 feet. Test at the $\alpha = .05$ level of significance to determine if the average length of the hoses is significantly different from what is advertised. Assume hose length is normally distributed.

SOLUTION:

Step 1. H_0: $\mu = 100$ (assumption to test)

H_0: $\mu \neq 100$ (2-tailed test).

Step 2. $\mu = 100$ (assumed)

$n = 25$ hoses (sample size)

$\overline{X} = 98.9$ feet (mean calculated from sample)

$s = 1.5$ feet (standard deviation calculated from sample)

$\alpha = .05$ (level of significance).

Step 3. The t-test is appropriate due to:

    1. Hose length is normally distributed in the population

    2. σ is unknown and s is used to substitute for σ

    3. $n < 30$.

Since we are using a two-tailed test (H_1: $\mu \neq 100$), the $\alpha = .05$ value will be divided equally into the two tails. Also, the t-distribution requires the calculation of degrees of freedom:

$$df = n\text{-}1$$
$$= 24.$$

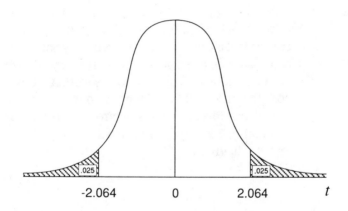

Therefore, $t = \pm 2.064$ according to the
Table of Areas for the Student's t-distribution.

Step 4.

$$t = \frac{\overline{X} - \mu}{s / \sqrt{n}}$$

$$= \frac{98.9 - 100}{1.5 / \sqrt{25}}$$

$$= -1.1/.3$$

$$= -3.67$$

Step 5. Since $|\text{-}3.67| > 2.064$, Rule A says that we should reject H_0 and accept H_1, which allows us to draw the conclusion that the manufacturer is probably not producing hoses with an average length of 100 feet. He should therefore adjust his process to ensure that the average hose length is 100 feet. There is however, up to a 5% chance that this decision is in error, i.e., $\alpha = .05$ is the probability that we have rejected a null hypothesis (H_0) that is actually true.

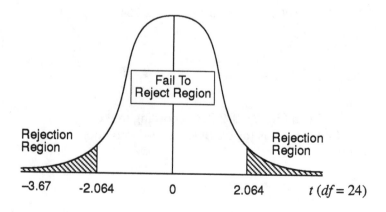

As with the Z-test, the t-test also allows for the determination of a decision based on a pictorial representation of the distribution. Here, we see, as indicated by Rule A, that the value t = -3.59 falls in the rejection region which is an indication that H_0 is to be rejected.

EXAMPLE 2:

The sales manager of the Wood Corporation assesses that the average number of miles traveled per week by the company salesmen is no more than 575 miles. In order to test this claim, a random sample of 15 salesmen is selected and it is determined that their mean average distance traveled per week is 600 miles. The standard deviation is also calculated and this value is 125 miles. If miles traveled is known to be normally distributed, test at the .10 level of significance to determine if the sales manager's claim is defendable.

SOLUTION:

Step 1. $H_0: \mu \leq 575$ (assumption to be tested)

$H_0: \mu > 575$ (1-tailed test).

Step 2. $\mu \leq 575$ (assumed)

$n = 15$ (sample size)

$\overline{X} = 600$ miles (mean calculated from the sample)

$s = 125$ miles (standard deviation calculated from the sample)

$\alpha = .10$ (level of significance).

Step 3.   The t-test is appropriate due to:

1. Miles traveled is normally distributed in the population.

2. σ is unknown and s is used to substitute for σ.

3. $n < 30$.

Since we are using a one-tailed test and the alternative hypothesis is $\mu > 575$, $\alpha = .10$ is placed in the right tail of the t- distribution. Also, the t-distribution requires the calculation of degrees of freedom:

$$df = n\text{-}1$$
$$= 14.$$

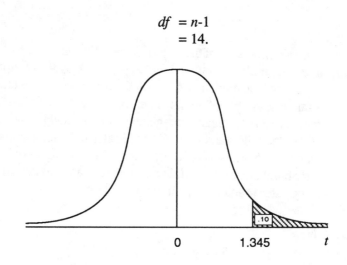

Therefore, $t = 1.345$.

Step 4.

$$t = \frac{\overline{X} - \mu}{s / \sqrt{n}}$$

$$= \frac{600 - 575}{125 / \sqrt{15}}$$

$$= 25 / 32.3$$

$$= .775$$

92

Step 5.   Since .775 < 1.345, Rule B says that we cannot reject H_0. There is not sufficient evidence from this sample to allow us to conclude that the claim made by the sales manager is unjustified. Again, as with the Z-test, the probability that this conclusion is in error is a value that must be calculated and is beyond the scope of the material in this text.

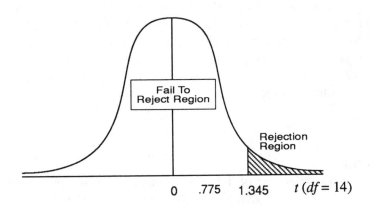

This graphic representation also supports Rule B. The computed t-statistic falls within the fail-to-reject region, indicating that we cannot reject H_0, based on the evidence at hand.

7.4   HYPOTHESIS TESTS ON PROPORTIONS

Another very common use of hypothesis testing deals with tests of proportions. In this situation, our interest is in testing to determine if the proportion of the population having a certain characteristic is as we assumed it to be; i.e., equal to some prespecified value. The procedures outlined previously for tests involving means apply for proportions, except for the small sample case. When testing proportions, the exact test for a sample size less than 50 is based on the binomial distribution. This procedure, however, is beyond the scope of the material presented in this text. Tests on proportions involve testing the relationship between two population proportions. The latter situation will be presented in *The Essentials of Business Statistics II*.

a. Testing That the Population Proportion is a Prespecified Value - Large Sample.

As we saw in confidence interval estimation, the Central Limit Theorem tells us that the sampling distribution of p (the sample percentage) is normally distributed when n > 50 and both $n\Pi$ and $n(1-\Pi)$ are greater than five. Therefore, when these conditions hold, we may apply the Z-statistic in hypothesis testing, just as we applied the Z-statistic in confidence interval estimation. The same five steps apply as used previously in testing of means.

EXAMPLE 1:

A manufacturer of light bulbs guarantees to his customers that at most 5% of the bulbs which he ships will be defective. A customer randomly selects 200 light bulbs from his shipment and tests to determine if any are defective. He finds 16 defective bulbs. Test at the .05 level of significance to determine if the manufacturer's guarantee is justified

SOLUTION:

Step 1. H_0: $\Pi \leq .05$ (assumption to be tested,
H_1: $\Pi > .05$ (1-tailed test).

Step 2. $\Pi \leq .05$ (assumed)

n = 200 (sample size)

16 = number of defective light bulbs in the sample

p = 16/200 = .08 (percentage of defectives in sample)

α = .05 (level of significance).

Step 3.   The appropriate distribution is the standard normal distribution (Z) due to:

1. $n \geq 50$

2. $n\Pi = 200(.05) = 10$

3. $n(1-\Pi) = 200(.95) = 190$.

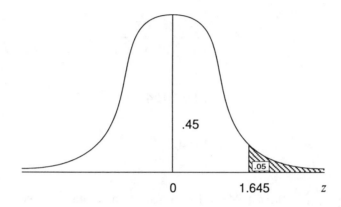

Therefore, $Z = 1.645$.

Note that $\alpha = .05$ is placed in the right tail of the curve. This is due to the fact that the alternative hypothesis carries the > sign.

Step 4.

$$Z = \frac{P - \Pi}{\sigma_p}$$

where: $\qquad \sigma_p \sqrt{\Pi(1 - \Pi)/n}$

$$Z = \frac{.08 - .05}{(.05)(.95)/200}$$

$$= .03/.0154$$

$$= 1.948.$$

Step 5. Since 1.948 > 1.645, Rule A indicates that we should reject H_0 in favor of H_1. This concludes that the manufacturer's guarantee is not justified; i.e., the rate of defective items appears to be greater than what has been specified. However, there is a 5% ($\alpha = .05$) chance that our conclusion is wrong. As illustrated before, we may arrive at the same conclusion using the normal curve diagram.

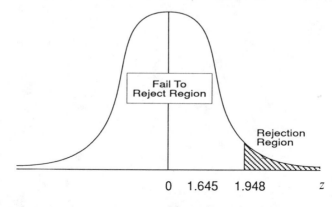

Fail To
Reject Region

Rejection
Region

0   1.645   1.948 z

Since 1.948 falls in the rejection region, we reject H_0 just as Rule A indicates.

EXAMPLE 2:

Federal Electronics conducted a random survey of 500 of their employees; 60% of this group indicated that the company was a good-to-excellent place to work. Company management had indicated prior to the survey that at least three-fourths of the employees would rate the company good to excellent. At the .01 level of significance, test to determine if management is correct in their assumption.

SOLUTION:

Step 1. H_0: $\Pi \geq .75$ (assumption to be tested)

                     H_1: $\Pi < .75$ (1-tailed test).

Step 2. $\Pi \geq .75$ (assumed)

                     $n = 500$ (sample size)

                     $p = .60$ (sample proportion)

                     $\alpha = .01$ (level of significance).

Step 3.   The appropriate distribution is the standard normal (Z) due to:

1. $n \geq 50$
2. $n\Pi = 500\,(.75) = 375$
3. $n(1 - \Pi) = 500\,(1 - .75) = 125$.

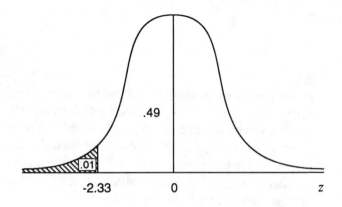

.49

.01

-2.33   0   z

Therefore, $Z = -2.33$, due to
the sign of the alternative hypothesis.

Step 4.

$$Z = \frac{P - \Pi}{\sqrt{\Pi(1 - \Pi)/n}}$$

$$= \frac{.60 - .75}{\sqrt{(.75)(.25)/500}}$$

$$= -.15/.01936$$

$$= -7.748$$

Step 5.   Since $|-7.748| > 2.33$, Rule A indicates that we should reject H_0 and accept H_1. The attitude of the employees is not as favorable toward the company as management had envisioned.

There is, however, a 1% chance that we have come to an incorrect conclusion. As shown, -7.748 is located in the rejection region indicating, as does Rule A, that the null hypothesis should be rejected.

7.5 TYPE I AND TYPE II ERRORS

As the previous sections have illustrated, hypothesis testing does not lead us to absolutely definite outcomes. Just because the result of the test is to reject H_0, or fail to reject H_0, we are not 100% sure that we have reached the correct conclusion. The same is true in confidence interval estimation, or in any other statistical inference technique. The explanation for this is that in inferential procedures, we are always working with sample data. And sample data can never yield definitive results due to the presence of sampling error.

Errors in conclusions drawn in hypothesis testing are referred to as either Type I or Type II. These are defined as:

Type I error - the decision to reject the null hypothesis (H_0) when it is true and should not have been rejected.

Type II error - the decision to fail to reject the null hypothesis (H_0) when it is false and should have been rejected.

The probability of making a Type I error is denoted by α (alpha) - the level of significance. As we have seen in previous examples, α is a pre-determined value which is specified in a textbook problem or in a real life type situation and is specified by the user(s) of the information. This is the chance that the user(s) of the information are willing to take that the null hypothesis might be rejected in error; i.e. that we might conclude that a difference or relationship exists when it really does not. The choice of this probability should consider the possible consequences of an incorrect decision. For example, in medical research where life sustaining situations are being tested, one would likely be much more conservative in specifying a value for α than in some of the examples presented herein. And even in critical business decisions, we would be very likely to set a conservative value for α.

The probability of making a Type II error is denoted by β (beta). This is not a predetermined value set by the user(s) of the information, but a value that can only be estimated once the result of the test is known. This procedure is not included in this text and, for the most part, is not of real concern to decision makers. The decision to fail to reject H_0 simply says that this particular sample does not provide enough evidence to support concluding otherwise. It is not a decision that is going to create life-threatening or devastating business situations. Many times it might, however, result in additional sample data being studied.

There are four possible outcomes in the decisions made from hypothesis testing. Two are in error and two are correct; they are easily illustrated in a table format as shown below.

H_0 **is**

		TRUE	**FALSE**
Decision from Test is to:	Reject H_0	TYPE I Error α	Correct Decision $1-\beta$
	Fail to Reject H_0	Correct Decision $(1-\alpha)$	TYPE II Error β

This table may be interpreted as follows. The null hypothesis (H_0) is either true or false. If it is true and our test leads us to say that it is not, we have committed a Type I error. The chance of this happening is α; therefore, the chance that we reach the correct conclusion would be $(1-\alpha)$. That is, we will either reach a correct or an incorrect conclusion and as we learned in elementary probability theory, the probability that an event occurs plus the probability that it does not occur sums to 1. By the same token, if H_0 is false and we fail to reject it, we have committed a Type II error and the probability that this will occur is β. Likewise, the probability that we reject H_0 when it is indeed false is $(1-\beta)$, using the same rationale.

Areas listed below*

Area under the Curve for the Standard Normal Distribution

$$z = \frac{X - \mu}{\sigma}$$

0   z

Z	.00	.01	.02	.03	.04	.05	.06	.07	.08	.09
0.0	.0000	.0040	.0080	.0120	.0160	.0199	.0239	.0279	.0319	.0359
0.1	.0398	.0438	.0478	.0517	.0557	.0596	.0636	.0675	.0714	.0753
0.2	.0793	.0832	.0871	.0910	.0948	.0987	.1026	.1064	.1103	.1141
0.3	.1179	.1217	.1255	.1293	.1331	.1368	.1406	.1443	.1480	.1517
0.4	.1554	.1591	.1628	.1664	.1700	.1736	.1772	.1808	.1844	.1879
0.5	.1915	.1950	.1985	.2019	.2054	.2088	.2123	.2157	.2190	.2224
0.6	.2257	.2291	.2324	.2357	.2389	.2422	.2454	.2486	.2518	.2549
0.7	.2580	.2612	.2642	.2673	.2704	.2734	.2764	.2794	.2823	.2852
0.8	.2881	.2910	.2939	.2967	.2995	.3023	.3051	.3078	.3106	.3133
0.9	.3159	.3186	.3212	.3238	.3264	.3289	.3315	.3340	.3365	.3389
1.0	.3413	.3438	.3461	.3485	.3508	.3531	.3554	.3577	.3599	.3621
1.1	.3643	.3665	.3686	.3708	.3729	.3749	.3770	.3790	.3810	.3830
1.2	.3849	.3869	.3888	.3907	.3925	.3944	.3962	.3980	.3997	.4014
1.3	.4032	.4049	.4066	.4082	.4099	.4115	.4131	.4147	.4162	.4177
1.4	.4192	.4207	.4222	.4236	.4251	.4265	.4279	.4292	.4306	.4319
1.5	.4332	.4345	.4357	.4370	.4382	.4394	.4406	.4418	.4429	.4441
1.6	.4452	.4463	.4474	.4484	.4495	.4505	.4515	.4525	.4535	.4545
1.7	.4554	.4564	.4573	.4582	.4591	.4599	.4608	.4616	.4625	.4633
1.8	.4641	.4649	.4656	.4664	.4671	.4678	.4686	.4693	.4699	.4706
1.9	.4713	.4719	.4726	.4732	.4738	.4744	.4750	.4756	.4761	.4767
2.0	.4772	.4778	.4783	.4788	.4793	.4798	.4803	.4808	.4812	.4817
2.1	.4821	.4826	.4830	.4834	.4838	.4842	.4846	.4850	.4854	.4857
2.2	.4861	.4864	.4868	.4871	.4875	.4878	.4881	.4884	.4887	.4890
2.3	.4893	.4896	.4898	.4901	.4904	.4906	.4909	.4911	.4913	.4916
2.4	.4918	.4920	.4922	.4925	.4927	.4929	.4931	.4932	.4934	.4936
2.5	.4938	.4940	.4941	.4943	.4945	.4946	.4948	.4949	.4951	.4952
2.6	.4953	.4955	.4956	.4957	.4959	.4960	.4961	.4962	.4963	.4964
2.7	.4965	.4966	.4967	.4968	.4969	.4970	.4971	.4972	.4973	.4974
2.8	.4974	.4975	.4976	.4977	.4977	.4978	.4979	.4979	.4980	.4981
2.9	.4981	.4982	.4983	.4983	.4984	.4984	.4985	.4985	.4986	.4986
3.0	.4987									
3.5	.4997									
4.0	.4999									

101

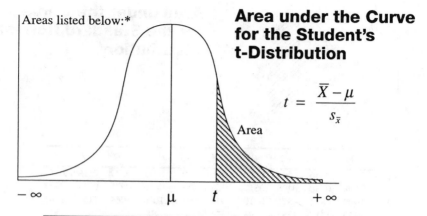

Areas listed below:*

Area under the Curve for the Student's t-Distribution

$$t = \frac{\overline{X} - \mu}{s_{\overline{x}}}$$

Area

$-\infty$ μ t $+\infty$

df	0.10	0.05	0.025	0.01	0.005
1	3.07	6.314	12.706	31.821	63.657
2	1.886	2.920	4.303	6.965	9.925
3	1.638	2.353	3.182	4.541	5.841
4	1.533	2.132	2.776	3.747	4.604
5	1.476	2.015	2.571	3.365	4.032
6	1.440	1.943	2.447	3.143	3.707
7	1.415	1.895	2.365	2.998	3.499
8	1.397	1.860	2.306	2.896	3.355
9	1.383	1.833	2.262	2.821	3.250
10	1.372	1.812	2.228	2.764	3.169
11	1.363	1.796	2.201	2.718	3.106
12	1.356	1.782	2.179	2.681	3.055
13	1.350	1.771	2.160	2.650	3.012
14	1.345	1.761	2.145	2.624	2.977
15	1.341	1.753	2.131	2.602	2.947
16	1.337	1.746	2.120	2.583	2.921
17	1.333	1.740	2.110	2.567	2.898
18	1.330	1.734	2.101	2.552	2.878
19	1.328	1.729	2.093	2.539	2.861
20	1.325	1.725	2.086	2.528	2.845
21	1.323	1.721	2.080	2.518	2.831
22	1.321	1.717	2.074	2.508	2.819
23	1.319	1.714	2.069	2.500	2.807
24	1.318	1.711	2.064	2.492	2.797
25	1.316	1.708	2.060	2.485	2.787
26	1.315	1.706	2.056	2.479	2.779
27	1.314	1.703	2.052	2.473	2.771
28	1.313	1.701	2.048	2.467	2.763
29	1.311	1.699	2.045	2.462	2.756
30	1.310	1.697	2.042	2.457	2.750
40	1.303	1.684	2.021	2.423	2.704
60	1.296	1.671	2.000	2.390	2.660
120	1.289	1.658	1.980	2.358	2.617
∞	1.282	1.645	1.960	2.326	2.576

Proportions of Area for the X^2 Distribution

Areas listed below:

For $df = 1.2$ For $df \geq 30$

df	0.005	0.010	0.025	0.050	0.100	0.500	0.900	0.950	0.975	0.990	0.995
1	7.88	6.63	5.02	3.84	2.71	0.455	0.0158	0.00393	0.0009	0.00016	0.00004
2	10.60	9.21	7.38	5.99	4.61	1.386	0.211	0.103	0.0506	0.0201	0.0100
3	12.84	11.34	9.35	7.81	6.25	2.366	0.584	0.352	0.216	0.115	0.072
4	14.86	13.28	11.14	9.49	7.78	3.357	1.064	0.711	0.484	0.297	0.207
5	16.75	15.09	12.83	11.07	9.24	4.251	1.61	1.145	0.831	0.554	0.412
6	18.55	16.81	14.45	12.59	10.64	5.35	2.20	1.64	1.24	0.872	0.676
7	20.28	18.48	16.01	14.07	12.02	6.35	2.83	2.17	1.69	1.24	0.989
8	21.96	20.09	17.53	15.51	13.36	7.34	3.49	2.73	2.18	1.65	1.34
9	23.59	21.67	19.02	16.92	14.68	8.34	4.17	3.33	2.70	2.09	1.73
10	25.19	23.21	20.48	18.31	15.99	9.34	4.87	3.94	3.25	2.56	2.16
11	26.76	24.73	21.92	19.68	17.28	10.34	5.58	4.57	3.82	3.05	2.60
12	28.30	26.22	23.34	21.03	18.55	11.34	6.30	5.23	4.40	3.57	3.07
13	29.82	27.69	24.74	22.36	19.81	12.34	7.04	5.89	5.01	4.11	3.57
14	31.32	29.14	26.12	23.68	21.06	13.34	7.79	6.57	5.63	4.66	4.07
15	32.80	30.58	27.49	25.00	22.31	14.34	8.55	7.26	6.26	5.23	4.60
16	34.27	32.00	28.85	26.30	23.51	15.34	9.31	7.96	6.91	5.81	5.14
17	35.72	33.41	30.19	27.59	24.77	16.34	10.09	8.67	7.56	6.41	5.70
18	37.16	34.81	31.53	28.87	25.99	17.34	10.86	9.39	8.23	7.01	6.26
19	38.58	36.19	32.85	30.14	27.20	18.34	10.65	10.12	8.91	7.63	6.84
20	40.00	37.57	34.17	31.41	28.41	19.34	12.44	10.85	9.59	8.26	7.43
21	41.40	38.93	35.4	32.67	29.62	20.34	13.24	11.59	10.28	8.90	8.03
22	42.80	40.29	36.78	33.92	30.81	21.34	14.04	12.34	10.98	9.54	8.64
23	44.18	41.64	38.08	35.17	32.01	22.34	14.85	13.09	11.69	10.20	9.26
24	45.56	42.98	39.36	36.42	33.20	23.34	15.66	13.85	12.40	10.86	9.89
25	46.93	44.31	40.65	37.65	34.38	24.34	16.47	14.61	13.12	11.52	10.52

df	0.995	0.990	0.975	0.950	0.900	0.500	0.100	0.050	0.025	0.010	0.005
26	11.16	12.20	13.84	15.38	17.29	25.34	35.56	38.89	41.92	45.64	48.29
27	11.81	12.83	14.57	16.15	18.11	26.34	36.74	40.11	43.19	46.96	49.64
28	12.46	13.56	15.31	19.93	18.94	27.34	37.92	41.34	44.46	48.28	50.99
29	13.12	14.26	16.05	17.71	19.77	28.34	39.09	42.56	45.72	49.59	52.34
30	13.79	14.95	16.79	18.49	20.60	29.34	40.26	43.77	46.98	50.89	53.67
40	20.71	22.16	24.43	26.51	29.05	39.34	51.81	55.76	59.34	63.69	66.77
50	27.99	29.71	32.36	34.76	37.69	49.33	63.17	67.50	71.42	76.15	79.49
60	35.53	37.43	40.48	43.19	46.46	59.33	74.40	79.08	83.30	88.38	91.95
70	43.28	45.44	48.76	51.74	55.33	69.33	85.33	90.53	95.02	100.40	104.20
80	51.17	53.44	51.17	60.39	64.28	79.33	98.58	101.90	106.60	112.30	116.30
90	59.20	61.75	65.65	69.13	73.29	89.33	107.60	113.10	118.10	124.10	128.30
100	67.33	70.06	74.22	77.93	83.36	99.33	118.50	124.30	129.60	135.80	140.20

Critical Values of F (Probabilities of 5 and 1 Percent)

degrees of freedom (numerator)

Each cell shows the 5% critical value (top) over the 1% critical value (bottom), written as 5% / 1%.

denom \ num	1	2	3	4	5	6	7	8	9	10	11	12	14	16	20	24	30	40	50	75	100	200	500	X
1	161 / 4,052	200 / 4,999	216 / 5,403	225 / 5,625	230 / 5,764	234 / 5,859	237 / 5,928	239 / 5,981	241 / 6,022	242 / 6,056	243 / 6,082	244 / 6,106	245 / 6,142	246 / 6,169	248 / 6,208	249 / 6,234	250 / 6,261	251 / 6,286	252 / 6,302	253 / 6,323	253 / 6,334	254 / 6,352	254 / 6,361	254 / 6,366
2	18.51 / 98.49	19.00 / 99.00	19.16 / 99.17	19.25 / 99.25	19.30 / 99.30	19.33 / 99.33	19.36 / 99.36	19.37 / 99.37	19.38 / 99.39	19.39 / 99.40	19.40 / 99.41	19.41 / 99.42	19.42 / 99.43	19.43 / 99.44	19.44 / 99.45	19.45 / 99.46	19.46 / 99.47	19.47 / 99.48	19.47 / 99.48	19.48 / 99.49	19.49 / 99.49	19.49 / 99.49	19.50 / 99.50	19.50 / 99.50
3	10.13 / 34.12	9.55 / 30.82	9.28 / 29.46	9.12 / 28.71	9.01 / 28.24	8.94 / 27.91	8.88 / 27.67	8.84 / 27.49	8.81 / 27.34	8.78 / 27.23	8.76 / 27.13	8.74 / 27.05	8.71 / 26.92	8.69 / 26.83	8.66 / 26.69	8.64 / 26.60	8.62 / 26.50	8.60 / 26.41	8.58 / 26.35	8.57 / 26.27	8.56 / 26.23	8.54 / 26.18	8.54 / 26.14	8.53 / 26.12
4	7.71 / 21.20	6.94 / 18.00	6.59 / 16.69	6.39 / 15.98	6.26 / 15.52	6.16 / 15.21	6.09 / 14.98	6.04 / 14.80	6.00 / 14.66	5.96 / 14.54	5.93 / 14.45	5.91 / 14.37	5.87 / 14.24	5.84 / 14.15	5.80 / 14.02	5.77 / 13.93	5.74 / 13.83	5.71 / 13.74	5.70 / 13.69	5.68 / 13.61	5.66 / 13.57	5.65 / 13.52	5.64 / 13.48	5.63 / 13.46
5	6.61 / 16.26	5.79 / 13.27	5.41 / 12.06	5.19 / 11.39	5.05 / 10.97	4.95 / 10.67	4.88 / 10.45	4.82 / 10.29	4.78 / 10.15	4.74 / 10.05	4.70 / 9.96	4.68 / 9.89	4.64 / 9.77	4.60 / 9.68	4.56 / 9.55	4.53 / 9.47	4.50 / 9.38	4.46 / 9.29	4.44 / 9.24	4.42 / 9.17	4.40 / 9.13	4.38 / 9.07	4.37 / 9.04	4.36 / 9.02
6	5.99 / 13.74	5.14 / 10.92	4.76 / 9.78	4.53 / 9.15	4.39 / 8.75	4.28 / 8.47	4.21 / 8.26	4.15 / 8.10	4.10 / 7.98	4.06 / 7.87	4.03 / 7.79	4.00 / 7.72	3.96 / 7.60	3.92 / 7.52	3.87 / 7.39	3.84 / 7.31	3.81 / 7.23	3.77 / 7.14	3.75 / 7.09	3.72 / 7.02	3.71 / 6.99	3.69 / 6.94	3.68 / 6.90	3.67 / 6.88
7	5.59 / 12.25	4.74 / 9.55	4.34 / 8.45	4.12 / 7.85	3.97 / 7.46	3.87 / 7.19	3.79 / 7.00	3.73 / 6.84	3.68 / 6.71	3.63 / 6.62	3.60 / 6.54	3.57 / 6.47	3.52 / 6.35	3.49 / 6.27	3.44 / 6.15	3.41 / 6.07	3.38 / 5.98	3.34 / 5.90	3.32 / 5.85	3.29 / 5.78	3.28 / 5.75	3.25 / 5.70	3.24 / 5.67	3.23 / 5.65
8	5.32 / 11.26	4.46 / 8.65	4.07 / 7.59	3.84 / 7.01	3.69 / 6.63	3.58 / 6.37	3.50 / 6.19	3.44 / 6.03	3.39 / 5.91	3.34 / 5.82	3.31 / 5.74	3.28 / 5.67	3.23 / 5.56	3.20 / 5.48	3.15 / 5.36	3.12 / 5.28	3.08 / 5.20	3.05 / 5.11	3.03 / 5.06	3.00 / 5.00	2.98 / 4.96	2.96 / 4.91	2.94 / 4.88	2.93 / 4.86
9	5.12 / 10.56	4.26 / 8.02	3.86 / 6.99	3.63 / 6.42	3.48 / 6.06	3.37 / 5.80	3.29 / 5.62	3.23 / 5.47	3.18 / 5.35	3.13 / 5.26	3.10 / 5.18	3.07 / 5.11	3.02 / 5.00	2.98 / 4.92	2.93 / 4.80	2.90 / 4.73	2.86 / 4.64	2.82 / 4.56	2.80 / 4.51	2.77 / 4.45	2.76 / 4.41	2.73 / 4.36	2.72 / 4.33	2.71 / 4.31
10	4.96 / 10.04	4.10 / 7.56	3.71 / 6.55	3.48 / 5.99	3.33 / 5.64	3.22 / 5.39	3.14 / 5.21	3.07 / 5.06	3.02 / 4.95	2.97 / 4.85	2.94 / 4.78	2.91 / 4.71	2.86 / 4.60	2.82 / 4.52	2.77 / 4.41	2.74 / 4.33	2.70 / 4.25	2.67 / 4.17	2.64 / 4.12	2.61 / 4.05	2.59 / 4.01	2.56 / 3.96	2.55 / 3.93	2.54 / 3.91
11	4.84 / 9.65	3.98 / 7.20	3.59 / 6.22	3.36 / 5.67	3.20 / 5.32	3.09 / 5.07	3.01 / 4.88	2.95 / 4.74	2.90 / 4.63	2.86 / 4.54	2.82 / 4.46	2.79 / 4.40	2.74 / 4.29	2.70 / 4.21	2.65 / 4.10	2.61 / 4.02	2.57 / 3.94	2.53 / 3.86	2.50 / 3.80	2.47 / 3.74	2.45 / 3.70	2.42 / 3.66	2.41 / 3.62	2.40 / 3.60
12	4.75 / 9.33	3.88 / 6.93	3.49 / 5.95	3.26 / 5.41	3.11 / 5.06	3.00 / 4.82	2.92 / 4.65	2.85 / 4.50	2.80 / 4.39	2.76 / 4.30	2.72 / 4.22	2.69 / 4.16	2.64 / 4.05	2.60 / 3.98	2.54 / 3.86	2.50 / 3.78	2.46 / 3.70	2.42 / 3.61	2.40 / 3.56	2.36 / 3.49	2.35 / 3.46	2.32 / 3.41	2.31 / 3.38	2.30 / 3.36
13	4.67 / 9.07	3.80 / 6.70	3.41 / 5.74	3.18 / 5.20	3.02 / 4.86	2.92 / 4.62	2.84 / 4.44	2.77 / 4.30	2.72 / 4.19	2.67 / 4.10	2.63 / 4.02	2.60 / 3.96	2.55 / 3.85	2.51 / 3.78	2.46 / 3.67	2.42 / 3.59	2.38 / 3.51	2.34 / 3.42	2.32 / 3.37	2.28 / 3.30	2.26 / 3.27	2.24 / 3.21	2.22 / 3.18	2.21 / 3.16
14	4.60 / 8.86	3.74 / 6.51	3.34 / 5.56	3.11 / 5.03	2.96 / 4.69	2.85 / 4.46	2.77 / 4.28	2.70 / 4.14	2.65 / 4.03	2.60 / 3.94	2.56 / 3.86	2.53 / 3.80	2.48 / 3.70	2.44 / 3.62	2.39 / 3.51	2.35 / 3.43	2.31 / 3.34	2.27 / 3.26	2.24 / 3.21	2.21 / 3.14	2.19 / 3.11	2.16 / 3.06	2.14 / 3.02	2.13 / 3.00
15	4.54 / 8.68	3.68 / 6.36	3.29 / 5.42	3.06 / 4.89	2.90 / 4.56	2.79 / 4.32	2.70 / 4.14	2.64 / 4.00	2.59 / 3.89	2.55 / 3.80	2.51 / 3.73	2.48 / 3.67	2.43 / 3.56	2.39 / 3.48	2.33 / 3.36	2.29 / 3.29	2.25 / 3.20	2.21 / 3.12	2.18 / 3.07	2.15 / 3.00	2.12 / 2.97	2.10 / 2.92	2.08 / 2.89	2.07 / 2.87
16	4.49 / 8.53	3.63 / 6.23	3.24 / 5.29	3.01 / 4.77	2.85 / 4.44	2.74 / 4.20	2.66 / 4.03	2.59 / 3.89	2.54 / 3.78	2.49 / 3.69	2.45 / 3.61	2.42 / 3.55	2.37 / 3.45	2.33 / 3.37	2.28 / 3.25	2.24 / 3.18	2.20 / 3.10	2.16 / 3.01	2.13 / 2.96	2.09 / 2.98	2.07 / 2.86	2.04 / 2.80	2.02 / 2.77	2.01 / 2.75
17	4.45 / 8.40	3.59 / 6.11	3.20 / 5.18	2.96 / 4.67	2.81 / 4.34	2.70 / 4.10	2.62 / 3.93	2.55 / 3.79	2.50 / 3.68	2.45 / 3.59	2.41 / 3.52	2.38 / 3.45	2.33 / 3.35	2.29 / 3.27	2.23 / 3.16	2.19 / 3.08	2.15 / 3.00	2.11 / 2.92	2.08 / 2.86	2.04 / 2.79	2.02 / 2.76	1.99 / 2.70	1.97 / 2.67	1.96 / 2.65
18	4.41 / 8.28	3.55 / 6.01	3.16 / 5.09	2.93 / 4.58	2.77 / 4.25	2.66 / 4.01	2.58 / 3.85	2.51 / 3.71	2.46 / 3.60	2.41 / 3.51	2.37 / 3.44	2.34 / 3.37	2.29 / 3.27	2.25 / 3.19	2.19 / 3.07	2.15 / 3.00	2.11 / 2.91	2.07 / 2.83	2.04 / 2.78	2.00 / 2.71	1.98 / 2.68	1.95 / 2.62	1.93 / 2.59	1.92 / 2.57

degrees of freedom (denominator)

Critical Values of F (Probabilities of 5 and 1 Percent)

Each cell shows the 5% critical value (top) and the 1% critical value (bottom).

df	1	2	3	4	5	6	7	8	9	10	11	12	13	14	15	16	17	18	19	20	21	22	23	24
19	4.38 / 8.18	3.52 / 5.93	3.13 / 5.01	2.90 / 4.50	2.74 / 4.17	2.63 / 3.94	2.55 / 3.77	2.48 / 3.63	2.43 / 3.52	2.38 / 3.43	2.34 / 3.36	2.31 / 3.30	2.26 / 3.19	2.21 / 3.12	2.15 / 3.00	2.11 / 2.92	2.07 / 2.84	2.02 / 2.76	2.00 / 2.70	1.96 / 2.63	1.94 / 2.60	1.91 / 2.54	1.90 / 2.51	1.88 / 2.49
20	4.35 / 8.10	3.49 / 5.85	3.10 / 4.94	2.87 / 4.43	2.71 / 4.10	2.60 / 3.87	2.52 / 3.71	2.45 / 3.56	2.40 / 3.45	2.35 / 3.37	2.31 / 3.30	2.28 / 3.23	2.23 / 3.13	2.18 / 3.05	2.12 / 2.94	2.08 / 2.86	2.04 / 2.77	1.99 / 2.69	1.96 / 2.63	1.92 / 2.56	1.90 / 2.53	1.87 / 2.47	1.85 / 2.44	1.84 / 2.42
21	4.32 / 8.02	3.47 / 5.78	3.07 / 4.87	2.84 / 4.37	2.68 / 4.04	2.57 / 3.81	2.49 / 3.65	2.42 / 3.51	2.37 / 3.40	2.32 / 3.31	2.28 / 3.24	2.25 / 3.17	2.20 / 3.07	2.15 / 2.99	2.09 / 2.88	2.05 / 2.80	2.00 / 2.72	1.96 / 2.63	1.93 / 2.58	1.89 / 2.51	1.87 / 2.47	1.84 / 2.42	1.82 / 2.38	1.81 / 2.36
22	4.30 / 7.94	3.44 / 5.72	3.05 / 4.82	2.82 / 4.31	2.66 / 3.99	2.55 / 3.76	2.47 / 3.59	2.40 / 3.45	2.35 / 3.35	2.30 / 3.26	2.26 / 3.18	2.23 / 3.12	2.18 / 3.02	2.13 / 2.94	2.07 / 2.83	2.03 / 2.75	1.98 / 2.67	1.93 / 2.58	1.91 / 2.53	1.87 / 2.46	1.84 / 2.42	1.81 / 2.37	1.80 / 2.33	1.78 / 2.31
23	4.28 / 7.88	3.42 / 5.66	3.03 / 4.76	2.80 / 4.26	2.64 / 3.94	2.53 / 3.71	2.45 / 3.54	2.38 / 3.41	2.32 / 3.30	2.28 / 3.21	2.24 / 3.14	2.20 / 3.07	2.14 / 2.97	2.10 / 2.89	2.04 / 2.78	2.00 / 2.70	1.96 / 2.62	1.91 / 2.53	1.88 / 2.48	1.84 / 2.41	1.82 / 2.37	1.79 / 2.32	1.77 / 2.28	1.76 / 2.26
24	4.26 / 7.82	3.40 / 5.61	3.01 / 4.72	2.78 / 4.22	2.62 / 3.90	2.51 / 3.67	2.43 / 3.50	2.36 / 3.36	2.30 / 3.25	2.26 / 3.17	2.22 / 3.09	2.18 / 3.03	2.13 / 2.93	2.09 / 2.85	2.02 / 2.74	1.98 / 2.66	1.94 / 2.58	1.89 / 2.49	1.86 / 2.44	1.82 / 2.36	1.80 / 2.33	1.76 / 2.27	1.74 / 2.23	1.73 / 2.21
25	4.24 / 7.77	3.38 / 5.57	2.99 / 4.68	2.76 / 4.18	2.60 / 3.86	2.49 / 3.63	2.41 / 3.46	2.34 / 3.32	2.28 / 3.21	2.24 / 3.13	2.20 / 3.05	2.16 / 2.99	2.11 / 2.89	2.06 / 2.81	2.00 / 2.70	1.96 / 2.62	1.92 / 2.54	1.87 / 2.45	1.84 / 2.40	1.80 / 2.32	1.77 / 2.29	1.74 / 2.23	1.72 / 2.19	1.71 / 2.17
26	4.22 / 7.72	3.37 / 5.53	2.98 / 4.64	2.74 / 4.14	2.59 / 3.82	2.47 / 3.59	2.39 / 3.42	2.32 / 3.29	2.27 / 3.17	2.22 / 3.09	2.18 / 3.02	2.15 / 2.96	2.10 / 2.86	2.05 / 2.77	1.99 / 2.66	1.95 / 2.58	1.90 / 2.50	1.85 / 2.41	1.82 / 2.36	1.78 / 2.28	1.76 / 2.25	1.72 / 2.19	1.70 / 2.15	1.69 / 2.13
27	4.21 / 7.68	3.35 / 5.49	2.96 / 4.60	2.73 / 4.11	2.57 / 3.79	2.46 / 3.56	2.37 / 3.39	2.30 / 3.26	2.25 / 3.14	2.20 / 3.06	2.16 / 2.98	2.13 / 2.93	2.08 / 2.83	2.03 / 2.74	1.97 / 2.63	1.93 / 2.55	1.88 / 2.47	1.84 / 2.38	1.80 / 2.33	1.76 / 2.25	1.74 / 2.21	1.71 / 2.16	1.68 / 2.12	1.67 / 2.10
28	4.20 / 7.64	3.34 / 5.45	2.95 / 4.57	2.71 / 4.07	2.56 / 3.76	2.44 / 3.53	2.36 / 3.36	2.29 / 3.23	2.24 / 3.11	2.19 / 3.03	2.15 / 2.95	2.12 / 2.90	2.06 / 2.80	2.02 / 2.71	1.96 / 2.60	1.91 / 2.52	1.87 / 2.44	1.81 / 2.35	1.78 / 2.30	1.75 / 2.22	1.72 / 2.18	1.69 / 2.13	1.67 / 2.09	1.65 / 2.06
29	4.18 / 7.60	3.33 / 5.42	2.93 / 4.54	2.70 / 4.04	2.54 / 3.73	2.43 / 3.50	2.35 / 3.33	2.28 / 3.20	2.22 / 3.08	2.18 / 3.00	2.14 / 2.92	2.10 / 2.87	2.05 / 2.77	2.00 / 2.68	1.94 / 2.57	1.90 / 2.49	1.85 / 2.41	1.80 / 2.32	1.77 / 2.27	1.73 / 2.19	1.71 / 2.15	1.68 / 2.10	1.65 / 2.06	1.64 / 2.03
30	4.17 / 7.56	3.32 / 5.39	2.92 / 4.51	2.69 / 4.02	2.53 / 3.70	2.42 / 3.47	2.34 / 3.30	2.27 / 3.17	2.21 / 3.06	2.16 / 2.98	2.12 / 2.90	2.09 / 2.84	2.04 / 2.74	1.99 / 2.66	1.93 / 2.55	1.89 / 2.47	1.84 / 2.38	1.79 / 2.29	1.76 / 2.24	1.72 / 2.16	1.69 / 2.13	1.66 / 2.08	1.64 / 2.03	1.62 / 2.01
32	4.15 / 7.50	3.30 / 5.34	2.90 / 4.46	2.67 / 3.97	2.51 / 3.66	2.40 / 3.42	2.32 / 3.25	2.25 / 3.12	2.19 / 3.01	2.14 / 2.94	2.10 / 2.86	2.07 / 2.80	2.02 / 2.70	1.97 / 2.62	1.91 / 2.51	1.86 / 2.42	1.82 / 2.34	1.76 / 2.25	1.74 / 2.20	1.69 / 2.12	1.67 / 2.08	1.64 / 2.02	1.61 / 1.98	1.59 / 1.96
34	4.13 / 7.44	3.28 / 5.29	2.88 / 4.42	2.65 / 3.93	2.49 / 3.61	2.38 / 3.38	2.30 / 3.21	2.23 / 3.08	2.17 / 2.97	2.12 / 2.89	2.08 / 2.82	2.05 / 2.76	2.00 / 2.66	1.95 / 2.58	1.89 / 2.47	1.84 / 2.38	1.80 / 2.30	1.74 / 2.21	1.71 / 2.15	1.67 / 2.08	1.64 / 2.04	1.61 / 1.98	1.59 / 1.94	1.57 / 1.91
36	4.11 / 7.39	3.26 / 5.25	2.86 / 4.38	2.63 / 3.89	2.48 / 3.58	2.36 / 3.35	2.28 / 3.18	2.21 / 3.04	2.15 / 2.94	2.10 / 2.86	2.06 / 2.78	2.03 / 2.72	1.98 / 2.62	1.93 / 2.54	1.87 / 2.43	1.82 / 2.35	1.78 / 2.26	1.72 / 2.17	1.69 / 2.12	1.65 / 2.04	1.62 / 2.00	1.59 / 1.94	1.56 / 1.90	1.55 / 1.87
38	4.10 / 7.35	3.25 / 5.21	2.85 / 4.34	2.62 / 3.86	2.46 / 3.54	2.35 / 3.32	2.26 / 3.15	2.19 / 3.02	2.14 / 2.91	2.09 / 2.82	2.05 / 2.75	2.02 / 2.69	1.96 / 2.59	1.92 / 2.51	1.85 / 2.40	1.80 / 2.32	1.76 / 2.22	1.71 / 2.14	1.67 / 2.08	1.63 / 2.00	1.60 / 1.97	1.57 / 1.90	1.54 / 1.86	1.53 / 1.84
40	4.07 / 7.31	3.23 / 5.18	2.84 / 4.31	2.61 / 3.83	2.45 / 3.51	2.34 / 3.29	2.25 / 3.12	2.18 / 2.99	2.12 / 2.88	2.07 / 2.80	2.04 / 2.73	2.00 / 2.66	1.95 / 2.56	1.90 / 2.49	1.84 / 2.37	1.79 / 2.29	1.74 / 2.20	1.69 / 2.11	1.66 / 2.05	1.61 / 1.97	1.59 / 1.94	1.55 / 1.88	1.53 / 1.84	1.51 / 1.81

(continued)

degrees of freedom (denominator)

Critical Values of F (Probabilities of 5 and 1 Percent)

degrees of freedom (numerator)

df (denom.)	1	2	3	4	5	6	7	8	9	10	11	12	14	16	20	24	30	40	50	75	100	200	500	∞
42	4.07 / 7.27	3.22 / 5.15	2.83 / 4.29	2.59 / 3.80	2.44 / 3.49	2.32 / 3.26	2.24 / 3.10	2.17 / 2.96	2.11 / 2.86	2.06 / 2.77	2.02 / 2.70	1.99 / 2.64	1.94 / 2.54	1.89 / 2.46	1.82 / 2.35	1.78 / 2.26	1.73 / 2.17	1.68 / 2.08	1.64 / 2.02	1.60 / 1.94	1.57 / 1.91	1.54 / 1.85	1.51 / 1.80	1.49 / 1.78
44	4.06 / 7.24	3.21 / 5.12	2.82 / 4.26	2.58 / 3.78	2.43 / 3.46	2.31 / 3.24	2.23 / 3.07	2.16 / 2.94	2.10 / 2.84	2.05 / 2.75	2.01 / 2.68	1.98 / 2.62	1.92 / 2.52	1.88 / 2.44	1.81 / 2.32	1.76 / 2.24	1.72 / 2.15	1.66 / 2.06	1.63 / 2.00	1.58 / 1.92	1.56 / 1.88	1.52 / 1.82	1.50 / 1.78	1.48 / 1.75
46	4.05 / 7.21	3.20 / 5.10	2.81 / 4.24	2.57 / 3.76	2.42 / 3.44	2.30 / 3.22	2.22 / 3.05	2.14 / 2.92	2.09 / 2.82	2.04 / 2.73	2.00 / 2.66	1.97 / 2.60	1.91 / 2.50	1.87 / 2.42	1.80 / 2.30	1.75 / 2.22	1.71 / 2.13	1.65 / 2.04	1.62 / 1.98	1.57 / 1.90	1.54 / 1.86	1.51 / 1.80	1.48 / 1.76	1.46 / 1.72
48	4.04 / 7.19	3.19 / 5.08	2.80 / 4.22	2.56 / 3.74	2.41 / 3.42	2.30 / 3.20	2.21 / 3.04	2.14 / 2.90	2.08 / 2.80	2.03 / 2.71	1.99 / 2.64	1.96 / 2.58	1.90 / 2.48	1.86 / 2.40	1.79 / 2.28	1.74 / 2.20	1.70 / 2.11	1.64 / 2.02	1.61 / 1.96	1.56 / 1.88	1.53 / 1.84	1.50 / 1.78	1.47 / 1.73	1.45 / 1.70
50	4.03 / 7.17	3.18 / 5.06	2.79 / 4.20	2.56 / 3.72	2.40 / 3.41	2.29 / 3.18	2.20 / 3.02	2.13 / 2.88	2.07 / 2.78	2.02 / 2.70	1.98 / 2.62	1.96 / 2.56	1.90 / 2.46	1.85 / 2.39	1.78 / 2.26	1.74 / 2.18	1.69 / 2.10	1.63 / 2.00	1.60 / 1.94	1.55 / 1.86	1.52 / 1.82	1.48 / 1.76	1.46 / 1.71	1.44 / 1.68
55	4.02 / 7.12	3.17 / 5.01	2.78 / 4.16	2.54 / 3.68	2.38 / 3.37	2.27 / 3.15	2.18 / 2.98	2.11 / 2.85	2.05 / 2.75	2.00 / 2.66	1.97 / 2.59	1.93 / 2.53	1.88 / 2.43	1.83 / 2.35	1.76 / 2.23	1.72 / 2.15	1.67 / 2.06	1.61 / 1.96	1.58 / 1.90	1.52 / 1.82	1.50 / 1.78	1.46 / 1.71	1.43 / 1.66	1.41 / 1.64
60	4.00 / 7.08	3.15 / 4.98	2.76 / 4.13	2.52 / 3.65	2.37 / 3.34	2.25 / 3.12	2.17 / 2.95	2.10 / 2.82	2.04 / 2.72	1.99 / 2.63	1.95 / 2.56	1.92 / 2.50	1.86 / 2.40	1.81 / 2.32	1.75 / 2.20	1.70 / 2.12	1.65 / 2.03	1.59 / 1.93	1.56 / 1.87	1.50 / 1.79	1.48 / 1.74	1.44 / 1.68	1.41 / 1.63	1.39 / 1.60
65	3.99 / 7.04	3.14 / 4.95	2.75 / 4.10	2.51 / 3.62	2.36 / 3.31	2.24 / 3.09	2.15 / 2.93	2.08 / 2.79	2.02 / 2.70	1.98 / 2.61	1.94 / 2.54	1.90 / 2.47	1.85 / 2.37	1.80 / 2.30	1.73 / 2.18	1.68 / 2.09	1.63 / 2.00	1.57 / 1.90	1.54 / 1.84	1.49 / 1.76	1.46 / 1.71	1.42 / 1.64	1.39 / 1.60	1.37 / 1.56
70	3.98 / 7.01	3.13 / 4.92	2.74 / 4.08	2.50 / 3.60	2.35 / 3.29	2.23 / 3.07	2.14 / 2.91	2.07 / 2.77	2.01 / 2.67	1.97 / 2.59	1.93 / 2.51	1.89 / 2.45	1.84 / 2.35	1.79 / 2.28	1.72 / 2.15	1.67 / 2.07	1.62 / 1.98	1.56 / 1.88	1.53 / 1.82	1.47 / 1.74	1.45 / 1.69	1.40 / 1.62	1.37 / 1.56	1.35 / 1.53
80	3.96 / 6.96	3.11 / 4.88	2.72 / 4.04	2.48 / 3.56	2.33 / 3.25	2.21 / 3.04	2.12 / 2.87	2.05 / 2.74	1.99 / 2.64	1.95 / 2.55	1.91 / 2.48	1.88 / 2.41	1.82 / 2.32	1.77 / 2.24	1.70 / 2.11	1.65 / 2.03	1.60 / 1.94	1.54 / 1.84	1.51 / 1.78	1.45 / 1.70	1.42 / 1.65	1.38 / 1.57	1.35 / 1.52	1.32 / 1.49
100	3.94 / 6.90	3.09 / 4.82	2.70 / 3.98	2.46 / 3.51	2.30 / 3.20	2.19 / 2.99	2.10 / 2.82	2.03 / 2.69	1.97 / 2.59	1.92 / 2.51	1.88 / 2.43	1.85 / 2.36	1.79 / 2.26	1.75 / 2.19	1.68 / 2.06	1.63 / 1.98	1.57 / 1.89	1.51 / 1.79	1.48 / 1.73	1.42 / 1.64	1.39 / 1.59	1.34 / 1.51	1.30 / 1.46	1.28 / 1.43
125	3.92 / 6.84	3.07 / 4.78	2.68 / 3.94	2.44 / 3.47	2.29 / 3.17	2.17 / 2.95	2.08 / 2.79	2.01 / 2.65	1.95 / 2.56	1.90 / 2.47	1.86 / 2.40	1.83 / 2.33	1.77 / 2.23	1.72 / 2.15	1.65 / 2.03	1.60 / 1.94	1.55 / 1.85	1.49 / 1.75	1.45 / 1.68	1.39 / 1.59	1.36 / 1.54	1.31 / 1.46	1.27 / 1.40	1.25 / 1.37
150	3.91 / 6.81	3.06 / 4.75	2.67 / 3.91	2.43 / 3.44	2.27 / 3.14	2.16 / 2.92	2.07 / 2.76	2.00 / 2.62	1.94 / 2.53	1.89 / 2.44	1.85 / 2.37	1.82 / 2.30	1.76 / 2.20	1.71 / 2.12	1.64 / 2.00	1.59 / 1.91	1.54 / 1.83	1.47 / 1.72	1.44 / 1.66	1.37 / 1.56	1.34 / 1.51	1.29 / 1.43	1.25 / 1.37	1.22 / 1.33
200	3.89 / 6.76	3.04 / 4.71	2.65 / 3.88	2.41 / 3.41	2.26 / 3.11	2.14 / 2.90	2.05 / 2.73	1.98 / 2.60	1.92 / 2.50	1.87 / 2.41	1.83 / 2.34	1.80 / 2.28	1.74 / 2.17	1.69 / 2.09	1.62 / 1.97	1.57 / 1.88	1.52 / 1.79	1.45 / 1.69	1.42 / 1.62	1.35 / 1.53	1.32 / 1.48	1.26 / 1.39	1.22 / 1.33	1.19 / 1.28
400	3.86 / 6.70	3.02 / 4.66	2.62 / 3.83	2.39 / 3.36	2.23 / 3.06	2.12 / 2.85	2.03 / 2.69	1.96 / 2.55	1.90 / 2.46	1.85 / 2.37	1.81 / 2.29	1.78 / 2.23	1.72 / 2.12	1.67 / 2.04	1.60 / 1.92	1.54 / 1.84	1.49 / 1.74	1.42 / 1.64	1.38 / 1.57	1.32 / 1.47	1.28 / 1.42	1.22 / 1.32	1.16 / 1.24	1.13 / 1.19
1000	3.85 / 6.66	3.00 / 4.62	2.61 / 3.80	2.38 / 3.34	2.22 / 3.04	2.10 / 2.82	2.02 / 2.66	1.95 / 2.53	1.89 / 2.43	1.84 / 2.34	1.80 / 2.26	1.76 / 2.20	1.70 / 2.09	1.65 / 2.01	1.58 / 1.89	1.53 / 1.81	1.47 / 1.71	1.41 / 1.61	1.36 / 1.54	1.30 / 1.44	1.26 / 1.38	1.19 / 1.28	1.13 / 1.19	1.08 / 1.11
∞	3.84 / 6.64	2.99 / 4.60	2.60 / 3.78	2.37 / 3.32	2.21 / 3.02	2.09 / 2.80	2.01 / 2.64	1.94 / 2.51	1.88 / 2.41	1.83 / 2.32	1.79 / 2.24	1.75 / 2.18	1.69 / 2.07	1.64 / 1.99	1.57 / 1.87	1.52 / 1.79	1.46 / 1.69	1.40 / 1.59	1.35 / 1.52	1.28 / 1.41	1.24 / 1.36	1.17 / 1.25	1.11 / 1.15	1.00 / 1.00

degrees of freedom (denominator)

"The ESSENTIALS" of
ACCOUNTING & BUSINESS

Each book in the **Accounting and Business ESSENTIALS** series offers all essential information about the subject it covers. It includes every important principle and concept, and is designed to help students in preparing for exams and doing homework. The **Accounting and Business ESSENTIALS** are excellent supplements to any class text or course of study.

The **Accounting and Business ESSENTIALS** are complete and concise, giving the reader ready access to the most critical information in the field. They also make for handy references at all times. The **Accounting and Business ESSENTIALS** are prepared with REA's customary concern for high professional quality and student needs.

Available titles include:

Accounting I & II

Advanced Accounting I & II

Advertising

Auditing

Business Law I & II

Business Statistics I & II

College & University Writing

Corporate Taxation

Cost & Managerial Accounting I & II

Financial Management

Income Taxation

Intermediate Accounting I & II

Macroeconomics I & II

Marketing Principles

Microeconomics

Money & Banking I & II

*If you would like more information about any of these books,
complete the coupon below and return it to us, or visit your local bookstore.*

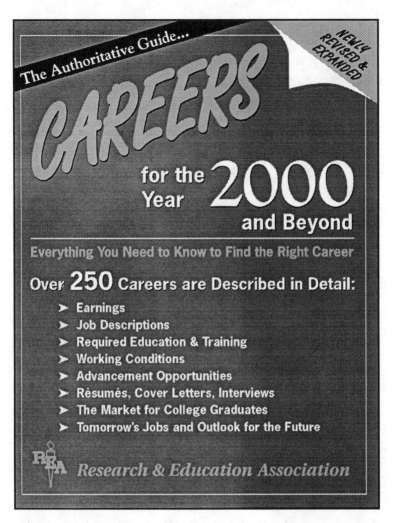